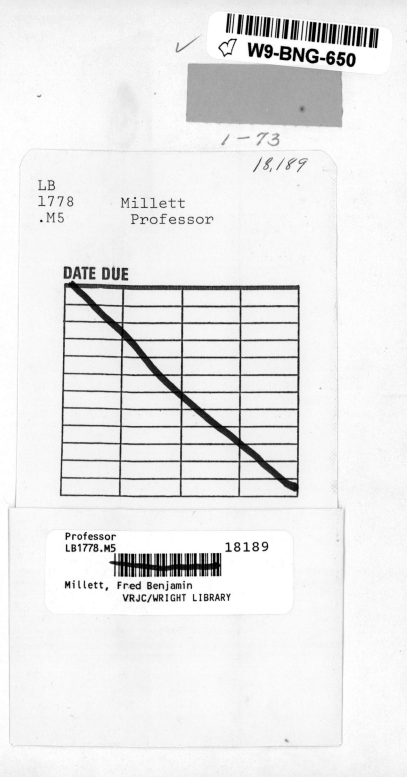

Macmillan Career Book

PROFESSOR

CAREER BOOK SERIES
Under Editorship of
Charles W. Cole

PROFESSOR by Fred B. Millett
LAWYER by Talbot Smith
PHYSICIAN by Dana W. Atchley (*preparing*)
ARCHITECT by Robert McLaughlin (*preparing*)
JOURNALIST by Herbert Brucker (*preparing*)

PROFESSOR

*Problems and Rewards in
College Teaching*

By FRED B. MILLETT

*The Macmillan Company
New York 1961*

First Printing

The Macmillan Company, New York
Brett-Macmillan Ltd., Galt, Ontario

Printed in the United States of America

Library of Congress catalog card number: 61-5386

Foreword

More than a quarter of a century ago, in the depression years, I interviewed a number of college seniors who were applying for fellowships to enable them to go on and do graduate work. Almost all of them had very firm notions about the kind of vocations they wished to pursue and how they thought they could best prepare themselves for the work they had in mind. Just recently, I had a similar opportunity to discuss the same subject with some fifteen seniors who were also candidates for fellowships. Only one of them had reached a really definite conclusion as to what he wanted to do. Most of them were hesitating between two, often unrelated, alternatives, while some were still considering three or four different possibilities.

During the last three decades I have talked to hundreds of young men about their career plans and their career decisions. I am sure that it is an accurate generalization that such plans and such decisions have become much more difficult to reach today than they were in the past. In part, the increasing difficulty arises from the obvious fact of the rapidly growing complexity of our society. There are literally hundreds of new callings, professions, and vocations, from airport traffic director and airline stewardess to hospital manager, business consultant, or television script writer—all unheard of thirty or forty years ago. Some old callings have disappeared. At the turn of the century every village had a blacksmith. Now it is hard to find one. At the same time many ancient professions have become more complicated, subdivided, and specialized. No longer does a young man merely decide to be a physician. He usually has to choose eventually among psychiatry, surgery, pathology, ophthalmology, pediatrics, cardiology, and a dozen other specialties.

Partly it has become harder to choose among careers today because, for many of them, not only is a college education required but also some training after the four-year college course is necessary or desirable. Many engineers take one or two years of graduate work beyond the bachelor's degree before beginning to practice their profession. Increasingly, young men who are planning to enter business go for one or two years to a graduate school of business administration, or perhaps substitute for that advanced work in accounting or economics. A high-school teacher used normally to have just a B.A. or a B.S. degree. Now most of them have master's degrees, and some have gone on to take the doctorate. Today many girls who are going into nursing take five or even six years in one combination or another of college and nursing school. To some degree it is an indication of how affluent our society is that so many young people can spend so many years in preparation for their lifework. But even more the prolongation of education arises from the needs and requirements of the most technically complicated society the world has ever seen.

Watching young men in college, I noticed a fact that seemed odd to me, an observation that is really the genesis of this Career Series. A good many students entering college think they have already chosen a life vocation. Most of those who plan to be physicians stick to that decision. But most of those who consider themselves pre-engineers abandon that idea during the four years. Even in the engineering schools that are most selective, the proportion of drop-outs and failures among the undergraduates is surprisingly high.

Why should premedical students differ from pre-engineering students in the firmness of their intentions and decisions? As I pondered this question and talked to students in both categories, the answer became utterly clear. The typical premedical student has a fairly well defined notion of what a doctor really does. He has been to a doctor's office. He has been to a hospital either as a patient or a visitor. He has read articles on the marvels of modern surgery and the new wonder drugs. In a biology class in secondary school he has already dissected a frog and a rat. And the idea of healing people, even by complex techniques, is basically a simple one.

The normal pre-engineering student, on the other hand, has only the vaguest understanding of what the work of an engineer is really like. Perhaps he thinks of it as mainly building bridges. He has no conception of the differences between chemical engineering, civil engineering, and aeronautical engineering. Nor does he realize that the most rigorous training in basic science and mathematics is part of the necessary equipment for an engineer. When, in college, he comes to a really difficult course like Differential Equations, he may suddenly discover that his aptitudes are more limited and his tastes less mathematical than he had thought. He reassesses his earlier decision and alters his career plan, but often with some lost motion and an impairment of his motivation.

Considering the problems in connection with career choices that all young men and women are facing, and realizing that what they needed most to help them was truly authentic information about the various professions and vocations, it seemed evident to me that a series like this one would be most useful. Discussion with a number of educators and guidance counselors confirmed the idea, and The Macmillan Company welcomed it as an opportunity to be of real service to young people in secondary school and college.

The plan for the series as it has developed calls for a limited number of books on the most important callings. Each is to be written by a person who has actually practiced and is intimately acquainted with the vocation in question, and who has achieved notable distinction in it. Each is designed to present in a thoroughly factual manner the problems of entrance into and practice of the different professions. But we hope the volumes will do more than that, for they are intended to give a vivid picture of what it is like to be a lawyer or a professor or an engineer or an architect. They will, moreover, endeavor to convey a sense of the personal requirements, the rewards, and the sacrifices involved in the various vocations. There will be no attempt to romanticize the professions or to heighten their color. What these books are designed to do is to help young people in the most practical possible way on one of the two most difficult decisions of life (the other being marriage).

In this volume Professor Millett discusses college teaching as a profession. He describes how one gets to be a professor, the necessary qualifications, intellectual and temperamental, the frustrations and the rewards of a career in higher education. In one chapter he describes in vivid detail what a professor's day may be like from dawn to long after dark. He is extraordinarily well qualified to write about professors, for he has spent half a century among them.

Dr. Millett graduated from Amherst College in 1912. He studied at Harvard and the University of Chicago and took his Ph.D. at the latter institution. He taught at Queen's University in Canada, the University of Chicago, the Carnegie Institute of Technology, and Wesleyan University. During the period of more than two decades when he was a member of the faculty at Wesleyan, he became Director of the Honors College and was known and respected as one of the most vital and effective teachers on the campus. Professor Millett has written a number of books and articles on English literature and the teaching of English and he has served on many committees and commissions connected with the teaching profession.

Though Professor Millett did much of his teaching in a small liberal arts college for men, he gives a sense of what university teaching is like and explains that the opportunities, life, and work of women professors closely parallel those of men. Because he loves teaching he sees clearly the problems, difficulties, and handicaps that a teacher faces. He resents, for example, the fact that the professor's salary has traditionally been inadequate in this country. But he is optimistic even in this regard, for he points out that the looming shortage of teachers will become so acute as to necessitate financial returns for teaching comparable with those of other professions.

He is, likewise, utterly clear on the joys of teaching—the give and take of the classroom, the delight of seeing a student's mind develop and grow, the opportunity to work in a field of one's own choice, the fact that a teacher is remarkably free to organize his own time and his own life, the excitement of intellectual discovery in research, the enduring thrill of living in a world of ideas. With all the allowances that have to be made for stupid students, unsatisfactory colleagues, overnumerous committees, bureaucratic administrators, and wearisome and repetitious routines, it is still true that the professor, more than almost everyone else, lives fully the life of the mind.

Though my own engagement in college and university teaching was less prolonged than that of Professor Millett, I can say with conviction that he has given a realistic picture of the profession. He is a little hard on administrators. He does not perhaps give full weight to the fact that the competitive conditions of the coming years are going to make the teacher's life more attractive in many ways. He is less concerned with science than with the humanities. But by and large he has been fair, thoughtful, and factual in describing what it is like to be a professor.

CHARLES W. COLE

AMHERST, MASSACHUSETTS
June, 1960

Contents

PROFESSOR

1

The Professor in America

If Arthur Bowditch Chadwick, Head of the Department of Economics at Harvard University in 1960, were to encounter his lineal ancestor, Asa Bowditch Chadwick, Professor of Greek and an influential member of the faculty in 1812, both men might find the meeting a little disconcerting. After they had given due attention to their family history, explored their common interests in teaching, in students, and in colleagues, and discovered that they combined a profound devotion to the university with a critical view of its president, they might not find it easy to hit upon other topics of conversation. The younger man might be a little put off by his ancestor's semiclerical attire, his decorous manner, and his measured, if not oracular, utterance. He might be astonished to learn that the older man had taught not only Greek but mathematics and Christian evidences. The older man might feel that his descendant's appearance could hardly be distinguished from that of a successful businessman and that his manner was informal, if not casual. He might be puzzled by the narrowness of the younger man's intellectual interests, his professional preoccupation not with the field of economics but with that of taxation, hardly, he might feel, a proper subject for university education. He would be even more bewildered by his descendant's absorption in the problems of administering his department, managing its complicated budget, planning elaborate schedules for his younger colleagues, and trying to fuse them into an effective and harmonious team of teachers and scholars. Both men would conclude that the Harvard of the early eighteenth century was vastly different from the Harvard of the mid-twentieth century and that the professor today, although moved by the same fundamental concerns as his predecessors, lives a very different life, with his obligations not only more varied but more onerous than those of his academic ancestors.

The purpose of this book is to discuss the training, the activities, and the responsibilities of the professor in twentieth century America. It will consider the factors that should enter into the basic decision as to whether or not a person should plan to become a professor. It will attempt to explain the various stages of his training in high school, college, and graduate school. It will describe the means by which the professor scales the academic ladder, and the various aspects of his professorial activity. Finally, it will strike a balance between the disadvantages and the advantages of college teaching as a profession, and describe the American professor's enduring rewards.

In the history of American higher education, there has never been a period when the doors of opportunity for college and university teachers have been as wide open as they are at present. The opportunity arises from the simple arithmetical fact that, as one educator put it, the depression babies, who were comparatively few in number, will be called on to teach the war babies, whose number showed a spectacular increase. In 1950 there were 2,659,000 college and university students in the United States. If the same proportion of Americans of college age continue to wish to go to college and can find a college to enter, it has been confidently predicted that the number of students will rise to four million or more by 1965, and to more than six million by

1970. Obviously, the demand for college and university teachers will accelerate proportionately.

There is no doubt that anyone who has any promise as a teacher and who has even a modest amount of training is going to be sought out by frantic college and university administrators. The need cannot be filled, moreover, although it may be mitigated, by extending the retirement age of competent teachers, by using the part-time services of experienced persons in industry and the professions, or by utilizing the talents of highly trained women after they have launched their own children toward adulthood. The demand for young persons who can be persuaded to embark on careers as college teachers is bound to be overwhelming.

It is also obvious that the graduate schools will be utterly incapable of turning out enough Doctors of Philosophy to satisfy the tremendous demand. In 1950, 6,633 Doctor's degrees were awarded; in 1954, 8,895. The estimate of the number of Doctors of Philosophy that would be needed, if even the present proportion of teachers with degrees (40 per cent) were to be maintained, varies from eight to ten thousand in 1965 and ten to fourteen thousand in 1970. It will no longer be possible to demand the Doctor's degree as a prerequisite for elevation on the academic ladder. It is further clear that teachers will be so urgently needed that every means will be devised to attract them by offering increasingly satisfactory salaries and by making their conditions of work as attractive as possible by freeing them from some of the nonpedagogical responsibilities they now bear. They will also be given student assistants and whatever mechanical aids may be available so that they may devote themselves solely to teaching, thus making more effective their conduct of the increasingly larger classes they will be asked to serve.

The college professor appeared in America within a few decades after the settlement of the Colonies. Harvard College was founded in 1636, William and Mary in 1693, and Yale in 1701. The founding of Princeton dates from 1746 and of Columbia from 1754. Inevitably, the American Colonial college took its model from the English colleges of which the early colonists had been graduates. Even the names of the four undergraduate classes into which the student body was conventionally divided were adapted from the English college system: freshman, sophomore, junior sophister, and senior sophister. The English college was a residential unit, with a few professors, a number of tutors, and a small student body. It was not, however, an isolated institution of higher education as the first colleges in the Colonies inevitably were. At universities like Oxford and Cambridge, the college was one of a considerable number forming a federation with a common governing body, the university. The small non-coeducational liberal arts college in America today offers the closest analogy to the American Colonial college.

The primary function of the American Colonial college was the preparation of students for the ministry, although, from the beginning, it also served as a steppingstone to the other learned professions, law and medicine, and to entrance into the higher levels of political and governmental activity.

For a century or more, the admission requirements consisted of the ability to read and to write Greek and Latin prose and verse. The curriculum was prescribed for all students; it consisted of the body of knowledge that was deemed sufficient and necessary for a liberally educated person. The curriculum was not designed to promote the discovery and dissemination of new truths, but to impart to the student the truths that had already been discovered. The faculty assumed that "there was a fixed and known body of knowledge—the liberal arts as they had come down from antiquity via the Middle Ages, Renaissance, and Reformation. This constituted absolute and immutable truth, and it was important that it be absorbed—not criticized or questioned—by every student." * As late as the middle of the eighteenth century, when the students at Yale took up a subscription to make possible the publication of John Locke's *Essay on Toleration*, the president threatened to withhold the degrees of the students involved unless they confessed their error in promoting this project.

The truths that the faculty devoted itself to communicating to the student body were embodied in courses in Greek, Latin, mathematics, natural philosophy, that is, the sciences, and usually Christian theology. A professor in an early American college was supposedly equipped to teach all these subjects, and the first presidents of Harvard and Yale taught them to all the students. Later, as the student body grew, the president turned the teaching of the younger classes over to tutors, but he reserved to himself the privilege of teaching all the subjects in the curriculum to the members of the senior class. Toward the end of the nineteenth century, a professor in a small liberal arts college who taught geology, biology, and Christian evidences observed that he occupied not a chair but a settee.

The president and tutors of an American Colonial college assumed responsibility for every aspect of their students' lives: social, physical, and moral. For example, the Harvard College Laws of 1642 laid down regulations that concerned "promptness, attendance at classes and prayers, dressing, idling, fishing, gaming, dancing, gambling, swearing." With the faculty taking upon itself the responsibility for the detailed scrutiny of student behavior, it is no wonder that the students came to regard the faculty as their natural enemies, and expressed their frustration in periodic riots that sometimes

* For the facts in this chapter, I am indebted to John S. Brubacher and Willis Rudy's comprehensive and judicious *Higher Education in Transition: An American History* (New York: Harper and Brothers, 1958).

resulted in the death or serious injury of faculty, students, or townsmen. The diary of President Ashbel Green of Princeton records vividly the trials and anxieties provoked by student rebelliousness:

> *April 5, 1814.* There were crackers in the institution today, and the evening was a most painful one to me. We met in faculty in a room of one of the tutors, and determined to dismiss two or three of the students. . . .
>
> *April 6, 1814.* The faculty met in the evening, and a pistol was fired at the door of one of the tutors. I ought to be very thankful to God for his support this day.
>
> *January 19, 1817.* A very serious riot commenced, with the manifest intention of preventing the usual religious exercises of that sacred day. . . . A great deal of glass was broken; an attempt was made to burn the out-buildings, and the bell was rung incessantly.

The life of the president and tutors in an American Colonial college was not that usually associated with the traditional ivory tower.

The conception of education embodied in the American Colonial college was essentially static, but the dynamic forces that led to the settling of the American continent gradually brought about striking changes, intellectual and material. Probably the most basic change was the abandonment of the idea that all the truth necessary to a liberally educated citizen had been discovered for the belief that the discovery of truth was a never ending process and that the faculty of a college should devote itself not only to extending the boundaries of knowledge but also to encouraging their students in discovery and exploration. A corollary of this process was the abandonment of the view that any particular religious or political sect had achieved final wisdom for the view that the institution of higher education should manifest its belief in "the illimitable freedom of the human mind. For here," in the ringing words of Thomas Jefferson, "we are not afraid to follow truth wherever it may lead nor to tolerate error as long as reason is left free to combat it."

In terms of fields of knowledge, the most dramatic change between the American Colonial college and the modern institution of higher education has been the expansion, fragmentation, and specialization of the curriculum. The spectacular advance of the natural sciences, particularly in the nineteenth and twentieth centuries, has forced the colleges and universities to increase the number of subjects that they must offer. The natural philosophy of the original curriculum became the mother of all the sciences, physical and biological. The ancient languages and literature in Greek and Latin had to make room for the modern languages and literatures. English literature, which had been merely an object of interest and curiosity for the educated gentleman, ultimately became a conspicuous member of the family of college studies. As modern society became increasingly complex and problematical, economics and political science split off from history and became independent disciplines.

Along with the spectacular expansion in the curriculum and in response to developing intellectual, professional, and social needs came the creation of genuine universities, where the original undergraduate liberal arts college was surrounded, if not smothered, by graduate schools of law, theology, and medicine and of institutions devoted to specialized education: institutes of technology, agricultural colleges, schools of business administration, and teachers colleges.

As a result of these startling changes, the American professor found that he could no longer take all knowledge for his province. He discovered that if he were to maintain his position in the academic world, he must become a specialist; not only must he devote himself to one discipline, such as Latin, economics, or biology, but he must also become a specialist in some particular phase of the discipline that he had chosen. A further encouragement to specialization came as a result of the impact of German university education on American higher education. Germany was the first country in western Europe to encourage and develop formal graduate training and study in all the disciplines and to establish the conception of the university as a company of scholars devoted to the pursuit of truth in their respective disciplines. A corollary of this conception was the expectation that persons trained in graduate methods of research should be productive scholars; that is to say, they should, by publication, make available to the world of scholars the results of their own researches. In the century between 1815 and 1915, more than ten thousand American students passed through the halls of German universities, and of these more than half studied in the faculties of the liberal arts and sciences. For America, the conspicuous effect of this German impact was the creation of graduate schools clustering around the original undergraduate liberal arts college. For the individual professor, the most important result was that he was expected to pursue graduate study in his discipline until he had obtained the degree of Doctor of Philosophy. The inevitable consequence of this training was that he emerged as a specialist in some aspect of his discipline; the expectation was that he would become a productive scholar in his chosen field.

The increasingly complex structure of American colleges and universities and the development of graduate schools encouraged a corresponding complexity in the status structure of college faculties. The relatively simple faculty of the American Colonial college—the president and the tutors—gave way to a more elaborate and carefully defined hierarchy.

After the acquisition of a Doctor's degree became an almost inescapable condition of academic advancement, college and university administrators tended to discriminate between teachers with a degree and those without a degree or those in the process of obtaining one. It became a conventional feature of academic institutional life to distinguish between instructors and assistant professors, associate professors and professors, vulgarly called full professors. An instructorship then became the rank of graduates of liberal arts colleges who had begun their work for the Doctor's degree but had not completed it. Appointment to an assistant professorship was commonly deferred until the instructor had proved himself to be a satisfactory teacher and was at least on the verge of obtaining his degree or had indeed obtained it. In most institutions, the associate professorship was reserved for men who had had a considerable amount of teaching experience and seemed promising enough as research scholars to be promoted in due time to professorships. Appointment to an associate professorship normally carried with it the fringe benefit of academic tenure, that is, the right to hold an academic position till the normal retirement age. Variations on this status scale, of course, occur in the infinite variety of institutions of higher education in America, but the academic ladder just described may be regarded as the norm from which some institutions diverge in one or another respect.

There were also significant changes in the nature of the American professor's clients, the undergraduate student body. In the colonial period, the student body tended to be limited to the sons of the clergy and of the professional classes generally. But even the denominational colleges in America never prescribed specific doctrinal tests in religion for the granting of degrees, unlike Oxford and Cambridge, which, until relatively recent times, refused to admit students who

were not members of the Church of England. As democratic
theories took root in America, the restriction of higher education to a social and economic elite became intolerable,
and partly through idealism and partly as a result of competition for students the doors were opened to students of
more and more diversified social and economic backgrounds.
The earlier denominational colleges, chiefly concerned with
recruiting members for the clergy, drew from social levels
untouched by the older colleges and universities. The undergraduates at Williams College, founded to add to the number
of orthodox clergy, were described by Nathaniel Hawthorne
as "country graduates—rough, brown features, schoolmaster-
looking, half-bumpkin, half-scholar, in black ill-cut broad-
cloth. . . . A rough-hewn set of fellows from the hills and
woods in this neighborhood."

Throughout the latter half of the nineteenth century and
the first half of the twentieth, the demand for college education accelerated. Publicly owned institutions like the state
universities, which depended on state legislatures for their
existence, were sometimes required by law to admit graduates
of all accredited high schools within the state. In the mid-
twentieth century, the rise of the student population is
accelerating at a tremendous pace. From the beginning, American colleges, like English colleges, have provided scholarships
to make it possible for gifted but economically underprivi-
leged students to attend. It has become increasingly apparent,
however, that there are still very large numbers of promising
students who are denied the privilege of higher education
because of its rapidly mounting costs. Not only private philanthropic foundations but the national government have
come to see that generous aid to such students is not only
intellectually but socially desirable. As a result of the increased demand for higher education and of the slowly
increasing opportunities for talented students to embark on

such an education, the modern American professor in most colleges and universities finds that his students represent fairly accurately a cross section of American society.

With the increase in the size of the student body, the faculty was no longer able to carry the burden of supervising every aspect of the student's life, both in and out of the classroom. The American college has always tended to be even more paternalistic than the English college on which it was modeled; its paternalism offers the sharpest possible contrast to the European university's lack of concern for any aspect of the student's life except the intellectual. But gradually the faculty of an American college or university has had to relinquish its responsibility for the student's mode of living and behavior to members of the college administration, who may be members of the faculty but whose responsibility is not primarily pedagogical. College administrations have proliferated deans, each of whom is responsible for some aspect of the student's life. There has also been a steady growth in the sense of the college's responsibility not only for the student's behavior but for his physical and mental well-being. The result has been the multiplication of student services. The earliest of these nonintellectual concerns had to do with his physical well-being; the results were the development of Departments of Physical Education and the common requirement that undergraduates shall, for at least three years, engage in formal types of exercise or games, whether they want to or not. With the development of psychiatry, there has been an increased attention to the student's mental health. In most institutions students are admitted only after the most careful scrutiny of their academic promise; if they fail to achieve the level of performance that may be expected of them, the college is concerned to discover what psychological blocks prevent their meeting the Admission Office's expectations. In colleges and universities where fraternities and sororities are permitted, these societies assume the responsibility for housing and sometimes for feeding their members and for maintaining a degree of decorousness in individual and group behavior. These responsibilities, however, are delegated by the administration and the faculty to the student groups. Some member of the administration, a dean or assistant dean, usually not only serves as a liaison between the institution and the group but also exercises a supervisory function with respect to them.

The modern professor in America today, therefore, finds himself freed from many of the responsibilities that weighed heavily on the professor in Colonial America. His primary job consists of teaching and the concomitants of teaching: meeting classes, preparing lectures, setting examinations, reading papers, recording absences, and reporting the results of his students' work to the appropriate dean. He is expected to see to it that his students maintain a reasonable degree of decorum in the classroom. He may participate indirectly in student discipline if he is required to report class absences to the dean who is responsible for seeing that the institution's requirements as to class attendance are complied with.

The modes of teaching available to the professor in modern America differ very considerably from those in use by his predecessors. Almost the only method of instruction in the American Colonial college was the recitation, the systematic checking up on whether or not the student had read the assignment in the required text and understood it. This mode of teaching survives, if anywhere, in introductory courses in the foreign languages that still appear in the curricula of most American colleges and universities, since, at least until very recently, American high schools have been remiss in introducing many students to the elementary stages of language instruction. Later, as the size of the undergraduate body increased, the lecture became—as it still is and is likely increasingly to be—a popular mode of teaching. In the Middle Ages, it had been almost the only method possible, since, before the invention of printing, students had no texts of their own. In a world flooded with printed books, the lecture is something of an anachronism. At its worst, it is a device for telling the student what he is expected to know, and the best student is the one who takes the most faithful and accurate notes and memorizes them. At its best, the lecture may be a valuable synthesis of information relevant to the topic discussed, a synthesis that furnishes the student a short cut to information he would have neither the time nor the discrimination to assemble and to organize himself. Probably the most popular current method of teaching is class or group discussion. At its worst, the class discussion can hardly be distinguished from the old-time recitation; at its best, with a teacher proficient in the Socratic method of analysis and cross-examination, it may be one of the most exciting of classroom experiences. Other modes of teaching that have taken their places in the repertory of the modern college teacher are the tutorial and the seminar. The tutorial involves the meeting of the teacher and not more than a very few students. The limitation in numbers makes possible a freer give and take among the members of the group. The subject matter of the tutorial is likely to be a program of advanced reading in a somewhat limited field. The seminar is perhaps the most intellectually advanced of the modes of teaching available to the college teacher in modern America. Here, the size of the group is also limited, and each student is likely to be assigned a topic for research and to pursue this investigation under the direction of the teacher conducting the seminar. When he has completed his work on his project, he usually presents his results to the group that constitute the seminar, in the form of a paper, which then serves as a basis for discussion by the teacher and the other students in the group. In recent years, both the social sciences and the humanities, especially the visual arts, have been developing types of laboratory work that, with significant differences, approximate the methods and objectives of laboratory work in the physical and biological sciences.

The modern professor's secondary job—at least in a college—is research and the publication of the results of his research when they have reached the appropriate stage. The distribution of his time and energy between teaching and research will depend in part on the personality of the teacher and in part on the emphasis the institution he is serving puts on teaching or research. Ideally, teaching and research should constitute the modern professor's total responsibility to the institution he serves. Actually, however, since the academic institution is a complex social organization, most professors discover that they are expected to render some form of service to the organization itself. At the very least, he will be expected to appear in proper academic regalia at commencement and other institutional occasions. But almost no professor escapes from rendering institutional service as a member of one or more college or university committees. His only method of escape is to achieve the reputation of not being a good "committee man," and he can hardly risk getting such a reputation—at least until he has attained tenure. Bureaucracies like colleges and universities have a marked tendency to multiply functions and to appoint committees to carry out these functions or, more frequently, to consider the desirability of the functions and the best means by which others than the committee may carry them out. The modern American professor who endears himself to a college or university administration is definitely an organization man.

The professor in modern America also has responsibilities that lie beyond the classroom, the departmental office, and the committee room. He is a member not only of a company of scholars but also of a well defined social community. Normally, he is a husband and a father, and his family is one unit in a fairly complex social structure. Here, academic status takes on another dimension: there are academic communities where professors and their wives restrict their social life to other professors and their wives, associate professors entertain only associate professors, and so on down the "pecking scale." In any case, in even the simplest academic community there is likely to be a social boundary between the permanent members of the faculty and the probably impermanent members. Furthermore, the ethical standards of the American academic community are distinctly higher than those of non-academic communities. Professors in America are expected to behave as decorously as clergymen in sophisticated urban communities. If you hope to become and remain a professor in America, you will have to behave.

But the professor has a responsibility not only to his students, the institution, and the academic community but also to the field in which he is a specialist. His responsibility to his discipline will manifest itself in his devotion to his research and the publications that result from such research. But it is also advisable, if not incumbent upon him, to maintain satisfactory relations with other scholars in his field, wherever they may be. These contacts may take the form of professional correspondence with other specialists in his field; they will certainly take the form of membership in one or more learned societies relevant to his field. If he is academically ambitious or if he hopes to be called to some major academic institution, he may devote a very considerable amount of his time to participating in the administration and the political life of some learned society.

The modern American professor, unlike the professor in Colonial America, does not run much risk of losing his life at the hands of a riotous mob of students. He does run the

risk of losing his equanimity as he attempts to distribute his
energies in response to the demands made on him as a teacher,
scholar, administration man, a member of an academic community, a member of the society of scholars, and also as a
husband and a father.

2

The Prospective Professor

How is the young person who is facing the choice of a profession to decide whether or not he should plan to become a professor? The choice of a profession is as important a factor in a successful and happy life as the choice of a wife (or a husband); and, for a young person, the choice of either a profession or a wife (or husband) is made difficult by the large number of unknowns inevitably involved. In the first place, the young person may not know himself with any degree of accuracy or depth, and, in the second place, he may know comparatively little about the work that professors do or the kind of life they live. He will have had more opportunity to observe the careers and activities of doctors and lawyers, of clergymen and businessmen than those of professors, of whom he may never have seen a living example. It is the business of this book to attempt to explain how one becomes a professor and what the life of a professor is like. It is the object of this chapter to assist the young person in arriving at as intelligent as possible a decision as to whether or not he is suited to the life and work of a professor. Whether or not the life and work of a professor are suited to him he may not be able to decide until he has had some experience of that life and work. One trusts that in most cases the initial decision will prove to have been a wise one.

It may be helpful to point out certain interests and aptitudes that the young person may discover in himself and that may suggest that it would be appropriate for him to plan to become a professor.

The first requirement, I should say, of the person who might become a professor is an interest in books, since, no matter what subject the professor decides to teach, he will always be concerned with books, with reading them, teaching them, and writing them. An interest in books and reading is, therefore, absolutely essential. It ought not to be difficult for a young person to decide whether or not he has a profound and insatiable interest in books. In the modern world the young person, outside school hours, is bombarded with forms of communication other than books, namely, the radio, the moving picture, and television. If the young person finds himself dissatisfied and bored by what these mass media tempt him to waste his time on, and if he gets something more meaningful from books than from these, there is no doubt that he possesses intellectual curiosity.

It should be said at once, however, that it is not enough that the young person should be a reader. *What* he reads is quite as important as the fact that he is a reader. The tidal waves of printed matter that threaten to engulf modern man bring in floods of mediocre and sentimental and cheap books. To be addicted to the reading of comic books, for example, is not a reliable guide to one's aptitude for becoming a professor, although some distinguished professors have been known "to rest their minds" by reading detective stories. In other words, the reader should be interested not only in books but in good books. Almost inevitably, the young reader will not find it easy at first to distinguish between the second-rate and the first-rate; indeed, some experience of the second-rate may be needed to develop the power to distinguish the first-rate from it.

What is also of the utmost importance in the matter of reading is the fields in which one is interested in reading, for the nature of these fields may play a decisive part in determining the areas in which the professor will ultimately want to teach. The choice of fields of reading will depend finally on the interests that come naturally to the young reader. He will certainly have the experience of developing an interest in some such subject as the American Indian or deep-sea diving or the novels of Mark Twain, and discover before very long that he has exhausted or thinks that he has exhausted this interest and feels the urge to pass on to some other, more absorbing subject. But the general areas in which his serious reading falls may very well give him a hint as to whether, when he becomes a professor, he will be active in the field of the humanities (literature and the fine arts, philosophy, and religion), the social sciences (history, economics, and government), or the natural sciences, whether physical or biological, or mathematics.

If an interest in reading is one indication that a young person might well consider becoming a professor, a liking for study may constitute a second clue. Compulsory universal education up to the school-leaving age means inevitably that a very large proportion of the students in elementary and secondary schools have no real aptitude for book learning or genuine interest in it, submit ungraciously to what they are compelled to study, and encourage their teachers to entertain them by more or less legitimate classroom tricks. In any undifferentiated class, however, there are always a few souls who obviously take delight in learning and really enjoy studying.

Such a devotion to study may grow out of a student's need for self-approbation or his need to win the approval of his parents and his teachers. The devotion to study will become a pleasure when it results in a job well done or when it grows out of a vigorous and wide-ranging intellectual curiosity. This intellectual curiosity, which is the ultimate source of man's greatest cultural achievements, may manifest itself early in the tendency to raise questions about matters that fall within the range of the young person's experience, and not only to raise questions but to feel an irresistible urge to discover, if possible, the answers to the questions he has raised. Essentially, we find here the origin of the research for which the professor is to be trained and to which he will more or less conscientiously devote himself. It is here that a love of reading serious books will render invaluable service to the intellectually curious.

Not all the questions raised can be answered by discovering the appropriate books; if this were so, knowledge would become static and sterile, as in some decadent civilizations it has conspicuously become. Some questions can be answered only by an experiential study of nature and man and society, but the questioner, the prospective researcher, will save himself a fearful wastage of time and effort if he resorts to books to discover what is already known about the subject concerning which he has raised questions. To discover what is already known, to come upon the answers that are conventionally, if mistakenly, regarded as correct, the young student should show some aptitude for discovering the best sources of knowledge; in other words, he should manifest the beginnings of a facility for exploring the reference resources that libraries, public and private, have to offer him. He will, of course, resort to the professional assistance of reference librarians, but he will not be contented until he has investigated any resources that might yield valuable results.

Another possible indication of the young person's aptitude for the college-teaching profession is his ability to work consecutively and strenuously at intellectual tasks, without becoming bored or restive with relatively sedentary activity.

College students who have had a considerable opportunity to observe professors in action may be attracted to the profession by what strikes them as its relatively leisurely life, and persons unacquainted with academic life usually think of it as incredibly easy and soft. If the professor does not teach more than nine or twelve hours a week, as he is likely to do in really reputable institutions of higher learning, the college student may be led to think that such a work load is ridiculously small for a self-sustaining adult. The incurious student overlooks the facts that the classroom performance involves the expenditure of a very considerable amount of nervous energy, and implies the devotion of a good deal of time to one or another sort of preparation. What even the unobservant student may notice is that the professor is constantly faced with the task of reading, commenting on, and grading the student themes and essays and quizzes that accumulate at an appalling rate in the course of a semester. The professor's other responsibilities, as a research scholar and as a member of an academic community, combine with his teaching, his preparation for teaching, and the correction of papers, to make him a very hard-working individual, if he takes his obligations seriously. Unlike the office worker, the professor does not have a nine-to-five job. In fact, the professor may very well envy the office worker or the young executive when he takes the commuters' train to Suburbia. The professor has very few free evenings during his working week; instead, he devotes his evenings, not often to his family or his social obligations or pleasures but to preparation of the next day's lectures or the reading and grading of papers that students put pressure on him to return at the earliest possible moment. The effectively functioning professor, therefore, has to have a highly developed capacity for organizing his working time, in and out of class, and for distributing his energies wisely. The greater degree of freedom that the professor enjoys—as compared with doctors and lawyers, for instance, or business executives—to work at his own time and speed, and to evolve his own program of work over and beyond his tightly scheduled classes, is paid for by the multiplicity of his responsibilities and the need for ordering his time efficiently and distributing his energies judiciously, since there is no higher-up to tell him what to do and when he is supposed to do it.

Another possible clue to the intelligent choice of a profession is the young person's attitude toward his teachers. Almost every student is fortunate enough to come to know some teacher who seems to him attractive and praiseworthy. Almost every serious student during his high-school or private-school experience will have found some teacher whose personality is so engaging, whose mind is so stimulating, and whose interests and tastes are so contagious that he will unconsciously become a model for imitation and emulation. On any level, probably the most effective teaching takes place when a student comes into contact with a teacher with these gifts. At any stage of education, imitation plays a very important role and, within limits, can serve a very useful function. But, after all, an imitation remains an imitation, and there have been notable instances in the history of American education where a strong personality so imposed itself on its disciples that they aimed to become duplicates of it. The results were disastrous for both the disciples and their students, since the disciples never had any desire to emancipate themselves from the beloved bondage; their students, therefore, were condemned to listen to secondhand versions of what may have been an excellent original. The really valuable kind of imitation involves the assimilation of certain of the model's attitudes, methods of work, and devices of performance with the powers of the individual student; the result will be not an inferior reproduction of the original but an individual enriched by reason of the assimilation.

Finally, among possible indications that a young person may be suited to the life of a college teacher is a liking for people and for working with people. It is natural that a young student should like and enjoy the company of people of his own age; it may be difficult or impossible for him to forecast whether in ten or twenty or thirty years he will still be interested in young people of college age. The most influential and effective college teacher, however, will be a person who is sincerely interested in students, who is anxious to know them as distinct personalities, who believes in their potentialities, and who devotes himself to assisting those potentialities to flower. If a young person feels that some of these attitudes manifest themselves in his relations with his high-school classmates or his fraternity brothers, he may have reason to hope that, if he should become a college teacher, his interest in undergraduates will be perennial. To revive and strengthen this interest, there is the circumstance that, as is not the case with one's offspring, one is confronted by different students not only year after year but semester after semester, and the constant possibility of new contacts, although it emphasizes the poignant transience of teacher-student relations, renews one's hopes that next semester's classes will contain individuals of special promise and power.

I have attempted thus far to suggest some of the more general personal traits that might justify a young person, in the process of deciding on the nature of his life work, in thinking of himself as a potential professor. It now remains to discuss the first steps the young student might be well advised to take by way of preparation for a career as a college teacher.

Since the prospective professor will realize that his training to become a college teacher will involve his graduating from college and attending graduate school, he will, of necessity, be preparing himself in high school for admission to the kind of college in which he would like to do his undergraduate work. The student should decide as early as possible what sort of college or university he thinks he would like to attend. Most high-school students, however, do not find it easy to arrive at such a decision. In most instances, the difficulty in making a choice arises directly from the ignorance of the student and his family of the differences among colleges of the same type and even more between colleges and universities. To be sure, if the student comes of a family some members of which have attended college, he will have the advantage of such knowledge as they have retained of the colleges they have attended, but their knowledge may very well be limited and almost certainly biased. In any case, what was appropriate for the student's parents or his uncles or his aunts may not be appropriate for him. It behooves the student and his parents, therefore, to learn as much as they possibly can about colleges and universities that seem attractive and appropriate. Since college and university publicity may be somewhat sentimental and romantic, the student and his parents should check the claims of the academic public-relations office against the experience of trustworthy students who have attended the institution. They should also visit the institution or institutions in which the student is interested, attend classes, inspect the college's buildings and equipment, talk to students, and form some notion of the quality of the faculty and the student body. Such visitations are perfectly normal procedures with admissions officers, who will attempt to make the student's visit as agreeable and informative as possible if they consider him a desirable candidate for admission.

The decision as to the colleges or universities to which the student should apply for admission should be made on the basis of both the nature of the student and the nature of the institution under consideration. To simplify the possible choices, one may limit them to institutions, small or large, coeducational or noncoeducational, close to the student's home or remote from it. Despite the fact that each institution in any one or more of these categories will have its individual character, the student and his parents may very well arrive at an intelligent and reliable judgment as to the kind of institution that will be most suitable for a student of a particular type of personality. Students who are shy and socially unaggressive, who are noncompetitive, and who do not have a marked need for achievement may make a place for themselves more easily in a small liberal arts college than in a large university. Brilliant students who thrive on competition and have a conspicuous need for achievement are likely to find the atmosphere of a large university more stimulating and invigorating than that of a small college. Whether or not the student should attend a coeducational or a noncoeducational college should depend, I believe, on the degree of emotional maturity at which he has arrived when he is about to enter college. The high-school graduate who has shown a considerable progress toward emotional maturity, toward reasonably satisfactory relations with the other sex, may profit by the monastic sequestration of a noncoeducational college if he is inclined to choose one for its character and prestige. High-school graduates who have given evidence of rather slow progress toward emotional maturity may be further retarded in their development by sequestration in a noncoeducational college. Finally, there is no doubt in my mind that, theoretically, attendance at an educational institution remote from one's home is preferable to attendance at one close to one's home. There may, of course, be practical considerations that will determine the choice of an institution near the student's home, but in general the student's necessary emancipation from dependence on his parents will be furthered if he is not sufficiently near home to make frequent contacts with his early environment possible.

As the student and his parents will discover before they

have advanced very far in a consideration of an appropriate college, their conclusion, however wisely arrived at, is not the decisive element in the situation. Whether or not the student will gain admittance to the college of his choice depends on factors that are not within the control of either the student or his parents. The most important of these factors is the number of other students who would like to enter the particular college in the same year. In the spring of 1959, both Harvard University and Boston College reported that of the three thousand students who had applied for admission in the fall of 1959, only a thousand could be accepted by each of these institutions; in other words, two out of the three students who hoped to become members of the Class of 1963 at either Harvard or Boston College were frustrated of their hopes. There is overabundant evidence to support the view that competition for admission to college will become more and more intense in the near future and that even larger proportions of applicants to a particular college will be unable to enter the college of their choice. Therefore, the student and his parents would be wise to choose not one but preferably three colleges that the student considers he might like to attend. The student should then apply to each of these colleges in the hope that one of them will find room for him and that he will be reasonably happy there. If the student is so fortunate as to be admitted to two of the colleges of his choice, he will then be in the enviable position of being able to decide as wisely as possible which of the two seems likely to prove the more satisfactory.

In selecting two or three colleges to which to apply for admission, the student should, of course, discover what the particular requirements for admission are and what the costs of attendance are likely to be. In the main, requirements for admission to liberal arts colleges have been regularized, but the student should discover from the college in which he is interested or from his adviser in high school what requirements he must meet if he is to be considered for admission. As a result, the student will find himself taking what is commonly called a college preparatory course, which will usually involve work in English, history, mathematics, some other science, and a foreign language.

The requirement as to a foreign language should be taken very seriously, particularly by the prospective professor. Not taking it seriously may cost him a great deal of time and effort years later. When the prospective professor investigates the requirements for admission to graduate school and those for the degree of Doctor of Philosophy, he will discover that one of the normal requirements is a reading knowledge of French and German. Some graduate schools allow the substitution for one of these languages of Italian, Spanish, or Russian, but the conventional requirements for candidates in the fields of the humanities and the social sciences are French and German. The prospective professor, therefore, should choose the modern language he is to study in high school with this consideration in mind, and he should apply himself to the best of his ability to the acquisition of a knowledge of the language sufficient to make the reading of books and articles in the language a matter of no great effort and, if possible, an occasion for pleasure. It might further be said, however, that, unless the student expects to do graduate work in one of the modern languages, the graduate school is interested, not in the student's skill in speaking the language but in his reading skill, although the ability to speak a foreign language may turn out to be an asset in travel or at international meetings of scholars.

Most colleges will furnish estimates of the annual costs to students who spend modestly, moderately, or lavishly. It is almost certain, however, that the cost of a particular student's education is likely to exceed both the official and the

private estimate. Because the tuition paid by the student to
the college covers only a small part of the cost of his education to the college, it is certain that tuitions are going to be
raised again and again in order to contribute something ap-
proaching their share to the constantly increasing overhead
expense of operation of American colleges and universities.
In the process of investigating the probable cost of his education, the student should also discover what the college
may offer as means of lightening the financial burden his
education will impose on his parents. Every reputable college and university has a more or less substantially endowed
scholarship fund; and, if the economic status of the parents
justifies the assistance of scholarship aid, the student need
feel no embarrassment in applying for such aid from the
colleges of his choice. If he is a very promising candidate for
admission, he may find himself in the fortunate position of
being able to choose among the scholarship awards made to
him, although he may wisely decide to go to the college he
prefers even though it may not have offered him the greatest
financial assistance.

If it seems unlikely that the student will receive scholarship aid to equal or to exceed his tuition, and if he needs to
supplement what his parents can contribute toward the cost
of his education, he should attempt to discover what opportunities there are for part-time work at or near the college.
To contribute to the cost of one's education by doing part-
time work has become an accepted feature of American higher
education, and the student who takes on such work does not
run the risk of losing status by so doing. But, unless the assumption of such tasks is absolutely necessary, it would be
well if the student and his parents should consider whether
his college work may not suffer from the diversion of some
of his time and energy to part-time jobs. The student who
combines college work and part-time jobs successfully needs

not only vigor and energy but also the capacity for organizing his activities so that he will not neglect either of his obligations and become involved in situations where he cannot do satisfactorily what he is supposed to do. The robust and vigorous student, on the other hand, who carries part-time work that is either manual or physical may find it a relief from the verbalizations and the abstractions of the classroom.

The prospective professor in high school will, in all probability, engage in a considerable number of the outside activities that modern school life proliferates. So long as these outside activities do not supersede in interest and importance the student's real business, his formal education, there is every reason to hold that these activities may be valuable, in both the long and the short run. In the short run, the student will find that, wisely or unwisely, college Admissions Offices are definitely interested in his record, not only in scholarship but in extracurricular activities: the holding of class offices, journalistic or editorial work on the school's newspaper or the class annual; debating or dramatics, or prowess in one or more forms of athletics. Many colleges and universities, it must be said, are less interested than they should be in what one might call pure intelligences. Pure intelligences strike some admissions officers as "odd balls." For social and economic reasons, many colleges and universities are interested in finding students with good minds, satisfactory characters, solid economic status, and a devotion to nonintellectual activities. In the short run, and more legitimately, the pursuit of an interest in outside activities may very well lead to the development of powers and abilities that the student did not know that he had. In the long run, the cultivation of outside activities that have some intellectual content, for example, dramatics and debating, journalistic or editorial work, may contribute directly to the student's ultimate success as a professor. Even an interest in sports, if pursued in moderation, may encourage habits of exercise that will offset the essentially sedentary character of a professor's life.

Finally, in the days that the prospective professor spends in high school or private school, not only should he fulfill his academic requirements with as much scholarly distinction as possible but he should at least attempt to discover and define the areas of his deepest intellectual interest. Such discovery and definition will assist him in planning a program of college studies that may very well prove the basis of his later professional activity. He might, however, be warned that there are dangers in too early a definition and limitation of his intellectual interests; what, in his youth, seems likely to be of enduring interest may presently turn out to be a transient infatuation, induced perhaps by an unusually skillful and influential teacher. There is also some danger of the development of a negative attitude toward subjects that do not make an immediate appeal to him. Both high school and college should be periods of intellectual exploration and discovery; if a student sails through these seas with too precise a conception of his destination, he runs the risk of never calling at many an enchanted island that may lie a little off his precisely planned course.

3

College Days

The years that the prospective professor spends in what one hopes is the college or university of his first choice should, if rightly spent, become an exciting and revealing voyage of discovery, discovery of the world of knowledge and discovery of the world of self. To make this journey of discovery as meaningful and colorful as possible, the undergraduate should not enter upon it with too clearly defined a notion of his itinerary; he should keep the way open for the discovery of areas of interest of which perhaps he had hardly suspected the existence.

In terms of discovery, the college or university offers a large number of courses in the hope that some of them will stir the student's interest and entice him to pursue them. The usual requirement that the student during his first two years in college should pass a certain number of courses in each of the major fields of knowledge—the humanities, the social sciences, and the natural sciences—many students find irritating and annoying. The "distribution requirement" has its theoretical justification in the ground that the liberally educated person should have at least a modest amount of guided intellectual experience in each of these basic areas of knowledge. Less than a century ago, the problem of what a liberally educated man should know was vastly more simple than it is today. In the early American college and university, a man was expected to have a fairly thorough knowledge of a limited number of subjects: Latin and Greek language and literature, mathematics, natural philosophy, that is, science, and Christian theology. The tremendous advances in human knowledge, the social and economic problems intensified by the Industrial Revolution, and the development of a society based on large-scale production and distribution have multiplied subjects of study at such a rate that no single student could even sample all the subjects offered by the modern college or university. Consequently, the undergraduate is expected to have some experience, at least on an elementary level, with one subject or more in each of the areas of knowledge to which it has become customary to assign the subjects taught in college. In the humanities, he will select from such subjects as English literature and composition, the ancient and modern languages, philosophy, religion, music, and the fine arts. In the social sciences, he will choose from among history, economics, and government. In the natural sciences, he will choose one or more samples from biology, chemistry, physics, astronomy, psychology, or mathematics.

The undergraduate who is really concerned with getting a liberal education should regard the usual "distribution requirements" not as more or less unattractive obligations to be discharged as rapidly and as painlessly as possible but as opportunities to widen and extend his intellectual experience. If the student keeps his mind open to what the subjects he has to study have to offer, he may, to his own great surprise and ultimate profit and pleasure, find that a subject in which, initially, he felt no interest may prove to be the subject to the study and teaching of which he will decide to devote his life. Students who came to college expecting to prepare for admission to medical school may find themselves choosing English literature as a major; students who expected to major in French may prove to be more genuinely interested in history or government.

In any case, the student who entertains the notion that he may adopt college teaching as a profession should use his early years in college to lay as broad as possible a foundation for the specialized work that he is to do later. In every field specialization is the order of the day, and if the student should ultimately become a college professor he will discover that most of his energies are going to be devoted to the study and teaching of some particular section of his chosen field. But no subject can profitably be studied in a vacuum; significant and illuminating relations can be established between almost any two subjects. Some contact with literature, the fine arts, philosophy, religion, or science can widen one's conception of history and broaden and deepen one's understanding of it. Literature will become more significant if it is studied not in a vacuum but as rising out of and influenced by a cultural matrix to which human achievements in science and industry, philosophy and the fine arts all may be relevant. Victorian literature, for example, was profoundly influenced by the rise of the doctrines of Darwinism, properly or improperly understood. The philosophical doctrines of Friedrich Nietzsche, grossly misinterpreted, played a malign role in the development of Nazism.

In the early years of his undergraduate education, the student who thinks he may become a professor should consider carefully his equipment in the modern languages. As I observed in the preceding chapter, he will discover, when he comes to investigate the requirements for admission to candidacy for the degree of Doctor of Philosophy, that a reading knowledge of two modern languages, usually French and German, is the normal prerequisite for acceptance as a candidate. In any case, if the student has acquired a fairly reliable reading knowledge of one modern language in high school or private school, he would be very well advised to start the study of his second modern language, if possible, in his freshman year in college. The younger student is likely to be less impatient of the grind of learning declensions and conjugations, the rules of grammar, and the correct use of prepositions than the older student. The foresight implied in the early study of these modern languages will pay off in the end: the prospective professor will not find himself, when he wants to devote himself exclusively to work for his Doctor's degree, confronted with the tiresome and time-consuming job of getting up a reading knowledge of a foreign language that he has never studied or that he has barely begun.

Probably every liberal arts college or university requires that the undergraduate should concentrate his studies sufficiently in his years as an upperclassman to give him a major in a single subject. In fact, meeting the requirements for a major may occupy something like half the student's time during his junior and senior years. In terms of a professorial career, no decision arrived at during one's college days is so important as the choice of a major, a choice that will not only give form and direction to his undergraduate education but also, in all probability, determine the subject that he will pursue in graduate school and teach after he has left graduate school. Obviously, this decision should be reached only after the most careful thought and consideration. In making this decision, the student should consider two problems primarily: his interest in the subject and his aptitude for its study. The depth and extent of his interest in the subject are not factors that can easily be estimated or measured. One indication of the nature of one's interests is the ability of the subject not only to stir interest but to arouse curiosity, to evoke in one the desire to go beyond the limits of one's knowledge and, ambitiously, to learn "everything" that can be learned about it. Another indication of the extent of one's interest is curiosity not merely about one aspect of the subject, one period in history or literature, for example, or one phase of economics, such as taxation, or of government, such as political parties, but about all the aspects of the subject; for, although the professor will undoubtedly specialize in some one aspect of his subject, he will be expected, both as a graduate student and as a teacher, to have at least a basic knowledge of the total subject.

The undergraduate's decision as to the subject on which he is to concentrate is, as I have said, important and may turn out to be final; but, if as his college days come to an end, he concludes that he has made an unfortunate or unpromising decision, he need not fear that he has condemned himself to lifelong devotion to a subject that interests him less than some other subject in which a later interest has been aroused. If he arrives at the conclusion that he wants to concentrate on a different subject when he gets to graduate school, he may find that it will take him some time to catch up with the subject that he has chosen and that his progress toward his Doctor's degree will be slightly delayed. If, on the other hand, the subject he has abandoned is somehow related to the one he is substituting for it, his understanding and appreciation of the new subject may, in the long run, be deepened by his earlier studies. If, for instance, he has majored in literature and decides that he wants to shift to history, he will discover that his knowledge of literature will enrich very considerably his study of the periods out of which the literature grew. Even if he should decide to shift from literature to psychology, his literary studies may very well contribute to his understanding of certain types of psychology, since the great literary masters have been great psychologists. The philosopher Friedrich Nietzsche said that he had learned more psychology from the Russian novelist Feodor Dostoevski than from anyone else.

The upperclassman will have a further opportunity to extend his interests and possibly to discover new interests in the elective courses that he will find himself in a position to choose. Perhaps half his courses in his junior and senior years will be electives. Some of the electives he chooses from among those the college or university offers him may be subjects related to his major; other electives may very well be subjects that are remote from his major but that stir his curiosity. If he should become a college professor, he may discover, when it is too late, that his years in college were his last opportunity to study formally and under expert guidance any subject except the one that is going to furnish the basis for his life work. One of the most reliable guides to the choice of electives is simply one's interest and taste. If the student has had an amateurish but enthusiastic interest in music, for example, his college days may offer him his first and last opportunity to approach music systematically and to deepen his understanding and appreciation of this great art. Indeed, it should give him a chance, as the study of any one of the fine arts does, to clarify and purify his taste. It was Walter Pater, I believe, who said that the purification of taste comes about through a series of disgusts, that is, as one's taste improves, one comes to see the shoddiness and sentimentality of some of one's earlier enthusiasms. There is, however, no reason why one should be embarrassed by the memory of his early and ill-advised enthusiasms. In the process of growth, there are inevitably awkward and ungraceful periods. If the undergraduate has any aptitude for creativity, and if the college offers him the opportunity, he might do well to try his hand at some form of creative art, painting or sculpture, wood carving or print making. Even though his creative aptitude should turn out to be meager, the experience will give him at least an insight into the way in which the artist works and an understanding of the problems the artist faces in attempting to realize his vision through the refractory medium he has chosen to use. At the best, the undergraduate may find that he has discovered a mode of creativity that will furnish relief and give him delight through his nonprofessional cultivation of it during his professorial career. Creativity of any sort is a happy counterbalance to the predominantly critical activity characteristic of most such careers.

The undergraduate intent on a professorial career should, furthermore, take every advantage offered him to do work of as advanced a character as possible, work that will encourage him to study independently and to begin the acquisition of the techniques of scholarly research. The opportunities offered will depend on the educational policy and practice of the institution in which the student finds himself. Most institutions, however, give their more promising students a chance to participate in seminars or to pursue an independent study project that may involve the writing of a thesis. At least, the student is almost certain to be expected to write term papers in even some of the largest classes he takes. In fact, in some courses, the term paper may be the chief device for determining the quality of the student's accomplishment.

Both the term paper and the thesis should serve to initiate the student into the elements of scholarly research, and, if he profits by this experience, it will stand him in good stead both as a graduate student and as a college teacher; it will give him a method of working that will prove useful throughout his productive life. From the writing of term papers or an undergraduate thesis, the student should learn the basic elements of scholarly investigation: the satisfactory limitation and definition of a subject, the efficient means of collecting a meaningful and significant bibliography of books and articles relevant to his subject, a reliable technique of note taking, the importance of absolute accuracy in the copying and recopying of quotations, the fair presentation of evidence for and against the thesis he has chosen to defend, experience in distinguishing what it is pertinent to include and to exclude from the thesis, experience in organizing his material so that it will furnish the reader a clear and easily comprehensible pattern and design, practice in attaining clear, correct, and forceful expression of his ideas, the correct form for footnotes and bibliography, and the scrupulous proofreading of what he has written before he submits it to his mentor's scrutiny. He will be fortunate indeed if his faculty guide is conscientious enough to give the term paper or the thesis the attention that it deserves. The mentor's comments, if thoughtfully and discerningly given, are potentially an extremely important pedagogical device, and the mature student will be less concerned with the grade his teacher gives him than with learning from the latter's comments how to avoid errors in method or presentation into which his inexperience has led him.

The seminar may also give the student an opportunity to get some practice in the oral presentation of his material and his ideas, and for such practice he may later find himself profoundly grateful when he suddenly discovers himself on a platform confronting a group of students who expect him to talk clearly, coherently, and meaningfully. With this contingency in mind, the prospective professor might very well consider whether or not he should take courses in public speaking or oral English in order that he may have some expert direction in the use of his voice and his body and experience in appearing before an audience and organizing and expressing what he has to say in such a way that his audience may have little difficulty in grasping his meaning. Either in formal public-speaking courses or in the oral reports he may be asked to give in seminars, the student will discover, among other things, that oral communication, if it is to be effective, differs fundamentally from written communication. The eye can grasp the meaning of a far more complex style and concentrated form of expression than the ear can. The eye, too, is aided by the visual organizing device of the paragraph as the ear is not. Accordingly, oral expression probably requires more obvious devices of coherence, more solid bridges between one topic and the next than most written expression does. The student will realize from his own observation that, although what the professor says may be important, the way in which he says it also has its importance. Clarity of diction, ease of manner, variety of tone, differences in stress and emphasis, all are important elements in an effective lecture, and, if the student can begin to acquire some of these skills, he may find his ultimate introduction to teaching a far less trying experience than it otherwise might be.

In all probability, the student will find himself moved or encouraged to try one or more of the extracurricular activities that are a conspicuous feature of American college and university campus life. Such activities as sports managerships or the holding of official positions in student organizations may contribute indirectly to his professional effectiveness later through what he learns about dealing with people and about getting others to contribute to a team or organization and about ordering the distribution of his own time and energy. Other outside activities may contribute more directly to his later professional efficiency. Such activities are campus journalism, public speaking, debating, and dramatics. Which of these activities is most appealing and which it will prove most profitable to attempt will depend on the particular undergraduate, but their values to the future professor are obvious. The professor will spend a good deal of his time writing; the professor will spend a good deal of his time speaking. Whatever may improve his performance in either of these activities will obviously be valuable to him. The journalistic opportunities open to undergraduates are those connected with the campus newspaper and the campus literary magazine. As with every other student activity, the vitality of either the campus newspaper or the campus literary magazine ebbs and flows. It is a perennial undergraduate plaint that interest in outside activities is dying out, and, as I recall the state of affairs in colleges fifty years ago, I should agree that there is far less general interest in outside activities than there was in the days when Woodrow Wilson, as president of Princeton, complained that the side shows got more attention from the students than what was going on in the main tent. But, whether or not there is less undergraduate interest in outside activities than there used to be, it is notorious that the vitality of any student activity fluctuates widely from student generation to student generation. A good editor of a campus newspaper or literary magazine can bring about its renaissance, but, if the good editor should happen to be succeeded by a weak editor, the renaissance may prove to be very short-lived. But in whatever state the paper or the magazine may be, its existence offers the student interested in writing a chance to try himself out, to discover how deep the interest is, and to get judgments on what he has written or printed. It is obvious that the undergraduate journalist will glean from his experience something very different from what the undergraduate poet or short-story writer will glean. The professor may look back with gratitude to his experience in undergraduate journalism for what he has learned about the elementary problems of a respect for fact, simplicity and clarity of style, and verbal appropriateness. Another professor may be grateful for what he has learned about the basic problems faced by the poet or short-story writer from his own attempts at writing imaginative literature. Not the least valuable result of this experience may be his conclusion that he does not have the makings of a full-time or perhaps even a part-time imaginative writer. Such a conclusion, even though arrived at painfully early in life, may possibly save the professor from easy self-delusion and major disillusionment later.

I have already spoken of the profit in training and experience that the prospective professor may gain from courses in public speaking. From the allied outside activity of debating, the undergraduate who is so inclined may also profit. I personally feel that debating is the dreariest form of indoor entertainment that I have ever been forced to endure. Moreover, as it is frequently taught, with the stress on winning a debate by fair means or foul rather than on discovering the truth about an issue, it tends to produce sophists rather than persons concerned with arriving at conclusions by a rational weighing of the evidence. It is, however, unfair to judge any human activity by its less admirable results. Aside from the valuable experience of learning to speak on one's feet and learning to offset one's opponents' arguments effectively, the debater may learn the difference between what is and what is not evidence, the importance of precision in definition and of clarity in the statement of the question and supporting arguments, the elements of logic, the importance of appropriate stress and emphasis, and skill in thinking rapidly and purposefully.

A certain type of undergraduate may find work in dramatics more congenial and, therefore, more profitable. There is no question in my mind that a great many professors would be more effective performers on the lecture platform if they had had some dramatic experience as undergraduates. There are a great many things that the prospective professor can learn from even a modest amount of experience on the amateur stage. From this experience, he may begin to acquire a sense of being at ease in the presence of an audience; more significantly, he can get a feeling for audience response, and perhaps develop some skill in getting the kind of response he

wants and not the reverse of the response desired. The satisfaction that may arise from manipulating the audience so
that it will give him the response he wants may very well
gratify not only the actor but the professor. From his experience on the stage, the prospective professor will learn something valuable about the way in which he may use not only
his body but his voice. If he is well directed, he will discover
that his voice is a very flexible and resourceful instrument
and that he can get a wide range of effects with it. It is very
important for the prospective professor to learn that low
tones and subdued utterance may be more effective in holding the attention of his audience and keeping it from getting
restive than tense tones and a high-pitched and irritating utterance. From the learning and delivery of lines, he may acquire
some of the art of reading aloud, and he can draw on this experience when, in the course of his lectures, he finds it pertinent to quote passages at considerable length.

There are two other extracurricular activities that will not
win the undergraduate any campus honors but that will earn
him impressive dividends in his later professional life: buying books and reading books. I have already said that one
symptom of prospective professorship is an interest in reading. But the undergraduate should not only read but begin
to cultivate the habit of buying as many books as he can
afford to buy. At the beginning, he will probably not buy
very wisely, but the experience of buying books that soon
lose interest for him may in itself be salutary and educational.
The undergraduate would do well to buy books in a variety
of fields; in his later professional life his book buying will
probably be narrowly professional or specialized; before
the days of his specialization begin, he may lay the foundations of a library that represents a breadth of cultural interests that, later in life, he may look back on somewhat en-
viously.

But the undergraduate should cultivate the habit not only of buying books but of reading books, and not merely books in which assignments have been made or books suggested for supplementary reading but books that he quite simply *wants* to read. I have no patience with the undergraduate who says that he has no time to read books that have not been assigned. Even the best organized and most systematic undergraduate thoughtlessly wastes a considerable amount of leisure time. If he is really interested in reading, he can use some of his leisure time for reading books that interest him personally. I am convinced that in contemporary student bodies the proportion of students who take books out of the college or university library simply because they want to read them is shockingly small; of that small proportion, I should wager that a considerable number are headed for a kind of professional life in which reading will be not only a utility but a source of unending pleasure and relaxation. In this connection, the undergraduate should familiarize himself with the library that the college has at great expense and by expert thought assembled for the benefit of both students and faculty. A great deal can be learned from browsing in a library; certain books standing quietly on library shelves speak to one and ask to be read, and some important new intellectual or emotional experience may come from a response to the book's call.

But perhaps the most important event in one's college days is not so much the discovery of the world of the mind and the minds and personalities of one's faculty and student contemporaries as it is the discovery of oneself. By the time the student enters college, he should be mature enough to be able to observe himself and to analyze himself with a fair amount of objectivity. In college he has ample opportunity to measure himself on a scale with other selected students of his own age and substantially his own experience. The student's years as an underclassman may prove to be a somewhat trying experience if he has arrived on the campus with the exaggerated notion of his own intellectual gifts and capacities that he has been encouraged to entertain in a high school or private school where he has made an excellent record.

In his freshman year he will perhaps for the first time discover that he is competing with others who are quite as gifted as he is or even more gifted. The shock of discovering that he is not so intellectually gifted as he thought he was may be a difficult one for him to withstand, but it is better to discover one's limitations while one is an undergraduate than to delay the disheartening discovery until one is experiencing the even stiffer competition of the graduate school. But the undergraduate's self-discovery should not be merely intellectual; he should take advantage of his seclusion from the life of the world and his nonparticipation in the onerous process of earning a living, to discover not only his intellectual capacities but his basic emotional pattern. He should use this opportunity to compare the configuration of his own personality with those of his closest friends among his contemporaries and to see himself with as great a degree of clarity and objectivity as possible. However disconcerting some aspects of his self-discovery may be, and however astutely he may classify himself as a type of personality, introvert or extrovert, subjective or objective, inner directed or outer directed, he should never forget that he is an individual with a unique array of interests, aptitudes, and gifts and that his task in life is the realization of as many of his potentialities as he can manage. By the time the undergraduate receives his diploma, he should have such a clear-eyed view of himself that he will not have an exaggerated conception of his performance in graduate school or in his later professorial life.

4

The Training of a Scholar

The prospective professor, long before he has completed his undergraduate work, will have become aware of the fact that, if he is to look forward to a career in college teaching, it will be necessary for him to attend graduate school and to acquire at least a Master's degree. Furthermore, although in 1955 only 40 per cent of the teachers in colleges and universities held the degree of Doctor of Philosophy, his academic mentors will certainly encourage him to plan to acquire this degree, sooner or later. College and university presidents and chairmen of departments generally take the view that the persons whom they appoint must either have the degree or be working for it. They are inclined to feel that a young man should not be appointed to an instructorship unless he has taken at least a Master's degree, which may be regarded as a preliminary step to the attainment of a Doctor's degree. In other words, the utilitarian reason for going to graduate school is the securing of a Master's degree or a Doctor's degree but preferably both.

If the college graduate has no other reason for attending graduate school, he is likely to find the time and effort he expends there excessive and the work he does there boring and intellectually unrewarding. If, however, he envisages the purpose of the graduate school as seen by its administrators and faculty, he may be able to find in his experience a significance that is not merely utilitarian. The major, if not the sole, purpose of the American graduate school is the training of scholars. In other words, the faculty of a graduate school assumes that its graduates will be productive scholars in the fields in which they have chosen to specialize, and the faculty members of the graduate school devote themselves to giving their students the training most likely to produce the best possible scholars.

But how does the graduate school conceive of the productive scholar? Perhaps the most illuminating analogy may be drawn from that conspicuous product of modern culture, the scientist. There are, to be sure, applied scientists and pure scientists. The applied scientist, like the engineer, is concerned with applying his scientific knowledge to the solution of practical problems, the production of improved consumer goods, like automobiles and vacuum cleaners, or the discovery of improved ways of curing physical and social ills. The pure scientist, whose usual habitat is a university laboratory, is concerned with learning something that has hitherto been undiscovered. The discoveries that he makes may ultimately prove to have their utility; the pure scientist, however, is interested in reducing the range of what has been humanly unknown and extending the range of the humanly known. In the purity of his motivation, in his isolation from the predominantly utilitarian concerns of his fellow mortals, the pure scientist is a modern equivalent of the scholar in a mediaeval monastery.

The analogy that I have been developing is not really so farfetched as it may seem to be. Scholarship in the humanities and the social sciences is, in essence, the result of the attempt to apply the scientific method to these fields of knowledge. This attempt to apply scientific method to areas beyond the physical and the biological sciences, indeed to every area of human experience, including religion, arose in the German universities in the second half of the nineteenth century and occurred as a result of the tremendous successes won by the scientific method in the late eighteenth and nineteenth centuries and the results that came from the application of scientific discoveries to industry, results that transformed modern man's ways of working and of living. These spectacular successes encouraged students of the humanities and the social sciences to apply the scientific method to their own fields. They were certainly moved, also, by the tremendous prestige that had accrued to scientists, to attempt to restore their own prestige by themselves becoming scientists of a sort. The early successes won by German scholars drew generation after generation of American students to German universities in order to get the kind of training that would make them adept in applying the scientific method to their own field.

Finally, as American colleges and universities grew by leaps and bounds after the Civil War, graduate schools were superimposed on the already existing undergraduate colleges or, in such an instance as the Johns Hopkins University, were established as independent institutions. Presently, these graduate schools no longer had to depend for their staffing on products of the German universities; they felt themselves capable of training their own scholars to become members of their own growing staffs or to go out to spread the gospel of scholarship to less favored institutions. Gradually, the Doctor's degree developed so much professional prestige that colleges were frequently rated in terms of the proportion of the staff that held the degree, and the degree became almost indispensable for advancement in the academic world.

The primary purpose of the graduate school was, and is, not the training of its students to become college teachers but the training of its students to become productive scholars in their respective fields. But just what is meant by scholarship in the humanities and the social sciences? It is much easier to see what scholarship means in the biological and physical sciences than in the humanities and the social sciences. The scientist, that is, the scholar in the physical and biological sciences, is the man who has been trained to make discoveries and who goes on attempting to make them. The method in which he is trained in college and graduate school is the scientific method, the method that can be relied on, with devotion and luck, to discover something that has not hitherto been known. In essence, the scientific method is not a complicated business. It consists in the definition of a problem, the formulation of a hypothetical solution to the problem, and the accumulation, by observation and experimentation, of evidence that supports or does not support the hypothetical solution that is being tested. If the evidence against the hypothesis is stronger than the evidence in support of it, then another hypothesis has to be conceived, which in its turn is demonstrated or rejected on the basis of the accumulated evidence. If the truth of the hypothesis has been demonstrated, then a scientific discovery of major or minor importance has been made.

The scientific method has achieved, and is still achieving, such spectacular results in the physical and biological sciences, and it has accordingly acquired such prestige as a method of working, that few people nowadays would oppose its application to every field of knowledge, even philosophy and religion. But the application of the scientific method to the study of human behavior in the fields of economics, political science, and sociology is a much more complex business than its application to inanimate matter or to the simpler forms of organic life. It is, of course, possible to entertain the conception of the economic man, for example. Aristotle thought of man, primarily, as a rational political animal. But, while valuable results may be derived from such conceptions as the economic man or the political man, these conceptions are actually intellectual abstractions. There never was a human being who was merely and solely an economic man or a political man. Systems like Marxism, constructed on the assumption that the economic motive in man is primary, have, especially in their prognostic aspects, proved profoundly false to human experience. The social sciences, properly pursued, demand powers of intuition and of analysis that exceed the limits of what is precisely and exactly scientific.

The value of the scientific method to the study of philosophy and religion is severely limited. The philosophical assumption underlying the scientific method—even though many practicing scientists may not be aware of the assumption—is that that only is truth that can be demonstrated experimentally. Such an assumption, if logically sustained, makes it necessary either to reject philosophical and religious truth completely or to make some unsatisfactory compromise between scientific truth and philosophical or religious truth. Actually, of course, most scientists lead a more or less uncomfortable schizophrenic existence; in the laboratory they work in accordance with the scientific method; outside the laboratory they live in the light of some more or less rational and systematic philosophical or religious belief. The scientific method, to be sure, can render modest services to the forms of knowledge that we know as philosophy and religion; it can go a considerable distance in discovering facts about philosophers or religious teachers, in establishing reliable texts, in demonstrating influences and cross-influences, and in writing the history of philosophy or of religion. But the scientific method cannot go very far in the direction of establishing the validity of either philosophical or religious truth; methods other than the scientific must, of necessity, be used here.

In the fields of literature and the fine arts, the scientific method is of only secondary significance. In literature and the fine arts, as in philosophy and religion, one is concerned with values rather than with facts. The scientific method is indispensable for the establishment of facts relevant to literature and the fine arts; by itself it can render no assistance in the establishment of the value of specific works of literature or works of art. It cannot distinguish between a first-rate and a tenth-rate work of art. The establishment of values in these fields is the concern of aesthetics and of criticism, which is the practical application of aesthetics to the evaluation of specific works. Although attempts have been made to establish a scientific aesthetics, the attempts have been doomed to failure. Literary or aesthetic judgment is not a subject that lends itself to scientific investigation.

The application of the scientific method to the social sciences and the humanities is, then, of limited propriety and serviceability, and the recognition of the limitations of the scientific method and of the results that it can achieve is becoming more and more general. And yet the graduate schools, by and large, continue to devote themselves to training their students in the scientific method, probably because it is a simpler task than training their students in the more complex methods appropriate to such humanly and intellectually complex subjects as religion, philosophy, and the arts. This narrow conception of graduate-school training is perhaps the major reason why graduates of a genuinely liberal arts college find entering graduate school a distinctly trying experience. Another cause of the commonly experienced trauma is the contrast between the personal tone of the college, with its faculty's intimate concern with individual students, their personalities and their problems, and the impersonal tone of the graduate school, an impersonality that arises in part from the teacher-student ratio of the graduate school but more particularly from the graduate-school faculty's interest in research rather than in teaching and in the graduate student's potentialities as a scholar and not in his potentialities as a human being.

What, then, do we mean by research and scholarship in the humanities and the social sciences? Research, one may say, is the means of which scholarship is the end. The primary function of the graduate school is training its students in the materials and methods of research and in seeing to it that these students produce a thesis that will demonstrate that they have learned to exemplify the discovery of materials and the application of good methods. The materials of research in the humanities and the social sciences include both primary sources and secondary sources. The nature of the primary sources differs from subject to subject, but, in the main, they consist of the basic records relevant to the subject: manuscript or printed materials or, in the case of the visual arts, works of art themselves. Thus, in philosophy, literature, or music, the primary sources would be the manuscripts left by the author or the earliest printed editions of his works; in the fine arts they would be the artist's own productions in whatever medium and the manuscript or printed materials relevant to the life and times of the artist. The secondary sources would consist of whatever has been written about these primary sources and their creators, either in the period of their creation or since. The secondary sources constitute what, in the jargon of scholarship, is "the literature of the subject," and one of the responsibilities of the scholar is "keeping up with the literature of the subject." As a matter of fact, he may spend so much time keeping up with the literature of the subject that he may give increasingly little attention to the primary sources themselves, the literary works or the works of art. As scholars and scholarly journals multiply, the "literature" of the disciplines increases at a terrifying rate, and a specialist may devote a very considerable amount of the time that he sets aside for reading to what has been written about his special subject by scholars all over the world.

One of the most important features of graduate-school

training is the discovery and use of primary sources. If these primary sources take the form of manuscripts, the chances of discovering hitherto unknown manuscripts varies from subject to subject, from author to author. In the case of an author like Shakespeare, for example, the chance that a manuscript of one of his plays will ever come to light is infinitesimal, although there are scholars who believe that Shakespeare's handwriting can be seen in the manuscript of a play on the subject of Sir Thomas More. There is still the possibility, however, that Shakespeare's name may be discovered among the hitherto unseen legal records of the period. The American scholar Leslie Hotson will always be remembered as the man who found Shakespeare's name in a legal document that showed that he and others had been brought before a justice of the peace to swear that they would keep the peace with respect to certain other persons. Hotson also was sufficiently adroit to discover documents that threw an entirely new light on the circumstances that led to the death of Shakespeare's contemporary, Christopher Marlowe. With authors later than Shakespeare and Marlowe, the possibility of discovering manuscript records is very much greater. Manuscripts, though seemingly fragile and destructible, have an amazing longevity, probably because human beings value the written word highly. Letters, in particular, are always turning up in a trunk in some neglected attic where they have lain unnoticed for generations. The almost strictly modern curiosity about the personalities of authors has had effects on both authors and scholars. In at least some authors, a self-consciousness has been induced that encourages them to collect and preserve their own papers, and it is said that a collector of Thomas Wolfe material presented something like two tons of it to Harvard University, and an even larger amount of material relevant to the career of H. G. Wells has been acquired by the University of Illinois.

The secondary sources relevant to a scholarly investigation consist of the discussions of the subject that sometimes exist in manuscript but more frequently in the form of printed books or scholarly articles. It is one of the first responsibilities of an investigator to learn what has already been done on the subject of his study. To attain this knowledge and not to miss anything essential to the history of the study of the subject necessitates the cultivation of an intimate acquaintance with bibliography and bibliographical aids. It is important to familiarize oneself not only with the obvious and easily accessible holdings of a university library but also to ferret out obscure and relatively unknown materials. Scholarship in the humanities and the social sciences has developed at such a tremendous rate that on almost any subject of investigation bibliographies have been assembled by experts. It must be remembered, however, that a scholarly bibliography is, in a sense, already out of date when it is published. The ardent researcher, therefore, must supplement what he finds in a bibliography by a vigilant inspection of current scholarly journals in order that he may keep abreast of recent research that may concern the subject he is investigating. Moreover, although the undergraduate may have learned something of the technique of getting at a library's resources, he will find that he needs to refine his technique if the library is to yield up all its riches to him.

The graduate student will also be expected to refine whatever he has learned about the methods of research as distinct from its materials. He must learn the proper bibliographical forms, since both his research papers and his thesis will hardly be considered complete without a list of the works that he has consulted or from which he has quoted. He must acquire a dependable and systematic method of note taking, since the notes he takes will constitute the basic matter of the research paper or thesis. He must train himself in the highest degree of accuracy in the transcription of passages that he may wish to quote, and must always record clearly and completely the source of the quotation. Unless he makes a habit of recording information of this sort, he may find himself wasting precious time chasing down the source of a quotation, a source that he was certain he would remember but that it is extremely easy to forget. In the study of literature, and in biographical studies in every field, he may find it necessary to learn to distinguish between first and later editions of an author's works and he must develop a high degree of skepticism with respect to the fidelity of editions that succeed the author's final revision of his text. Skepticism indeed is an indispensable part of the scholar's equipment; he must train himself to be distrustful of anything he sees on the printed page unless there seems good reason to believe that it can be trusted. In our culture, the printed word is generally regarded with such excessive respect that the grossest errors in fact may go unchallenged for years until the properly skeptical reader comes along.

With these conceptions of the purpose and the methods of graduate study in mind, the undergraduate who decides to go to graduate school in order to acquire either an M.A. or a Ph.D. or both is still confronted with the very difficult problem of the choice of a graduate school to which he may apply for admission. The decision is not only important but difficult.

The undergraduate, in order to get some light on the solution of his problem, would be well advised to seek the advice of the members of the department in which he is majoring. He will naturally turn not merely to those he knows best but to those whom he admires most. He will not be surprised to discover that most of the faculty members whom he consults will probably recommend most highly the graduate school from which they have secured their own advanced degrees.

The choice of a graduate school raises the nice problem of measuring the prestige of one school against that of others, or, more accurately, measuring the prestige of a degree from a particular school against the prestige of a degree from other schools. This is really a problem in measuring the immeasurable, since prestige is a highly subjective phenomenon. Actually, the prestige of a degree, however estimated, has only a limited importance. Its importance is greatest at the point in the graduate student's career when he is seeking his first appointment as a full-time teacher. At this crucial moment in his career, a degree from a particular institution may open up to him a larger number of opportunities than a degree from another institution. Students from graduate schools whose degrees are national in their prestige may find that they have opportunities to teach in almost any part of the country in which they may care to teach. Students from graduate schools whose degrees are regional in their prestige may find that they are not likely to get an appointment outside the region where the influence of the graduate school is dominant. But the importance of the prestige of a degree is, I believe, limited to the graduate student's first appointment. Thereafter, the importance of the source of his degree diminishes rapidly; whether or not he stays at the first institution to which he is appointed or moves on to another better or worse institution depends, thenceforth, primarily on himself, his personality, his productivity, his success as a teacher.

The undergraduate might also inquire from informed persons what the teacher-student ratio is likely to be in the graduate school that he is considering. Although he may be disappointed in the amount of personal attention he gets from the graduate faculty, at least during his first two years in the graduate school, he may well consider how good his chances may be of getting the attention he would like from the authority who will guide his thesis. The rapid increase in the enrollment of most graduate schools that seems certain to mark the near future will make it more and more difficult for students to discover schools where they will get very much personal attention, even when they are ready to present their theses for consideration and judgment.

What the undergraduate should be interested in discovering by checking opinions against each other is the distinction of a particular department in a particular school that he thinks of attending and, less significantly perhaps, the strength of the department in the aspects of the field in which the undergraduate has already developed an interest. This latter consideration, however, should not be given too much weight, since it is a common experience for the graduate student's focus of interest to change during his early years in graduate school under the influence of his own awakened curiosity or the influence of some distinguished member of the department whose disciple he may feel it attractive to become.

The undergraduate aiming at graduate study should also make some comparison between the various schools' requirements for the Doctor's degree. Although there may be a high degree of conformity among programs of study for the Doctor's degree, there may be differences in terms of the areas required for study and in the emphasis on a general knowledge of the field and a knowledge of the specific field out of which the student's thesis will develop. In the field of English literature, for example, there may be significant variations in the emphasis put on knowledge of the earlier stages of the language in which the literature has been composed. Fifty years ago, two of the leading graduate schools in the country maintained that a reputable student who expected to teach English literature should have at least an Introduction to Sanskrit!

In the field of literature and the fine arts, in particular, there are some graduate schools that have modified considerably their conception of graduate training and of the dissertation that is to be its crowning accomplishment. The rise and influence of the New Criticism have resulted in the infiltration of some graduate departments by professors who are primarily interested in critical theory or in practical criticism, the application of critical theory to specific works. As a result, the graduate curriculum may very well offer courses in critical theory or in the intensive analysis of particular works; furthermore, in such schools the graduate student may be permitted to submit as a dissertation a critical rather than a historical treatment of his chosen subject. So conspicuous have been the results of this infiltration that one historically oriented English professor has been heard to complain that all Doctors' dissertations nowadays seem to be on Henry James, James Joyce, or William Butler Yeats!

The student considering the problem of the choice of a graduate school should also ascertain the various schools' requirements with respect to the publication of his dissertation. Formerly, the requirement that the dissertation be published at the student's expense was general, if not universal, and for publication a great deal was to be said, since published dissertations constitute the most reliable objective evidence of the quality of the work approved by a particular graduate school. A published dissertation also furnishes substantial evidence of the character of the training and the quality of the mind of the graduate student who has produced it. Probably the major reason for the relaxation of the requirement of publication has been the heavy financial burden that rising costs of printing and publication impose on the student at a time when he has probably exhausted his financial resources in maintaining himself during the years he has devoted to graduate study, research, and the writing of his dissertation. A secondary reason for the relaxation is perhaps the changing conception of the function of the dissertation. It was formerly held that the dissertation should be an indubitable "contribution to knowledge." Usually, a dissertation *is* a contribution to knowledge, but the size of the contribution is normally infinitesimal. In some quarters, therefore, the dissertation has come to be regarded as evidence that the student is able to handle the materials and methods of research and to apply them to a project of considerable size, even though the subject itself may not be of overwhelming significance. If the dissertation is so considered, there is no very good reason for its publication, since it will, at any rate, be available in typed form to those who wish to consult it in the university library. The requirement that, within a limited period, a significant portion of the dissertation shall be published in a journal or separately represents a more or less happy compromise between publication and nonpublication. Such a requirement and the subsequent distribution of the published effort to other universities at least ensures that other scholars may become aware of the fact that the subject of the dissertation has been treated and that the treatment may indeed be of use to them in their own labors.

In the final choice of a graduate school, there are two practical considerations that should not be overlooked. The first is the particular requirements for admission to the school in which the student has become interested; the other is the possibility of securing financial aid during one's years in graduate school.

The requirements for admission to a particular graduate school can be learned by consulting the catalogue of the graduate school, which can be secured by writing directly to its director of admissions or can be consulted in the undergraduate college's collection of catalogues in the dean's office or in the library. Although requirements for admission to graduate schools have been fairly well normalized, the undergraduate may discover, to his dismay, that the graduate school in which he is interested has unusual requirements. For example, most graduate schools will not admit students to candidacy for the Doctor's degree until they have demonstrated that they have a reading knowledge of French and German, but certain of the older graduate schools also require a reading knowledge of Latin. The undergraduate should discover the details involved in the mechanics of application: the form of the application, the date when it must be submitted, the nature of the supporting evidence, and the specific requirements as to achievement, such as the nature and character of his undergraduate work and the score he has made on the Graduate Record Examination. If he is required to submit his record on this examination, he should discover where and when it is given and take it early enough to ensure the result's being available when he submits his application for admission.

It would probably be well for the student to apply for admission to several graduate schools, since competition for admission to graduate schools with high prestige is so lively that he cannot be sure that he will be accepted by the graduate school of his first choice unless he has made a top-flight undergraduate record and can count on getting enthusiastic recommendations from his faculty sponsors.

The undergraduate aspiring to enter graduate school should exercise his maximum astuteness in the selection of the members of the faculty whom he is to ask to write recommendations for him. Some faculty members enjoy writing recommendations; some do not. Most faculty members, in writing recommendations, are inclined—as I believe they should be—to give students the benefit of the doubt, since an undergraduate may unexpectedly flower in the stimulating and competitive atmosphere of a graduate school. Others are so painfully honest that they cannot resist balancing a student's shortcomings against his strong points. In any case, in writing a recommendation, a member of the faculty is doing the student a very considerable favor; the recommendation may be decisive in the matter of his admission to the graduate school of his choice. The student, therefore, should make clear to his overburdened faculty sponsor that he really appreciates the favor that is being done him.

The prospective professor, unless he is unusually fortunate in his family's financial circumstances, will almost certainly be interested in the problem of financing his graduate education. He should, therefore, ascertain the possibility of his being given some form of financial aid by the graduate school of his choice. This aid may take the form of a scholarship that covers tuition, a fellowship that covers tuition and contributes to living costs, or appointment as a teaching assistant or a part-time teacher. It is rather unusual for a graduate school to award a fellowship or a teaching-assistantship to a person who has done no graduate work. Usually, the best that a recent graduate can expect is the award of a scholarship that will cover his first year's tuition.

Assistantships or teaching fellowships are fairly common in state universities where large numbers of instructors are needed in the freshman English course which thousands of entering students are required to take. The acceptance of an assistantship or a teaching fellowship inevitably slows down the process of getting an advanced degree, since the student will have to divide his energies between teaching and graduate study, and, if he takes his teaching seriously, his graduate courses are almost certainly bound to suffer. The only advantage the student derives from his experience as an assistant or teaching fellow is the acquisition of teaching experience, but this advantage is minor, since graduate faculties and prospective employers assume that a Doctor's degree is adequate insurance that its possessor is a good teacher!

On being admitted to graduate school, the student may be asked to decide immediately whether he will work for a Master's degree or start work for a Doctor's degree. In any case, he should ascertain the relationship between the requirements for these degrees. In some instances the program leading to the first degree will differ to such an extent from that leading to the more advanced degree that an early decision will be necessary. If the student decides to work for both a Master's degree and a Doctor's degree, he may discover that securing the lesser degree may slow down slightly his progress to the more important degree. Despite this consideration, the graduate student will, I believe, be well advised if he first sets his sights on the Master's degree. Securing this degree will furnish an outward and visible sign of the progress he is making in his graduate studies; indeed, it may prove to be a valuable anchor to windward if one or another circumstance—ill health, lack of funds, bad luck with the Doctor's dissertation —should delay his attainment of the major degree.

The program of study, the requirements in the way of courses and seminars which the graduate student will be expected to pass with some distinction, is designed to serve two purposes. The first purpose is to give the graduate student so broad a knowledge of the subject matter of his field that he will be equipped, as a teacher, to give at least introductory courses in any aspect or period of his subject. The second purpose is to lay the groundwork for his acquiring an intensive knowledge of some particular aspect or period of his field so that he may be equipped to work out a dissertation relevant to this aspect or period and ultimately become a specialist in it. Thus, he may look forward to the time when, as a teacher, he may offer advanced courses to undergraduates or graduate students in the aspect of his subject in which he has become something of an authority. Usually, the course requirements for the Doctor's degree are planned to occupy the first two years of graduate study; thereafter, freed from specific course requirements, the graduate student may devote himself to the production of his dissertation.

The graduate student will very soon discover that the courses and seminars on his program differ very considerably from those that he has taken as an undergraduate. The subjects of the courses and seminars will be treated far more seriously and searchingly than those he has studied in college. The emphasis, naturally, will be on a scholarly—indeed a scientific—approach to the subject. In the courses the student takes, the graduate teacher will attempt to synthesize the existing knowledge of the subject, will contribute what he can from his own discoveries in the field, and will encourage the student to attempt to extend the boundaries of that knowledge by making new, if not spectacular, discoveries of his own. The reading assigned for the course is almost certain to include not only the relevant primary texts but also the most valuable secondary sources in the form of scholarly books and articles. The tone of the lectures is likely to be more impersonal and formal than any the undergraduate has been accustomed to hearing. The intellectual atmosphere is more rarefied. The writing the student does for his courses will almost certainly take the form of short or long exercises in the treatment of scholarly problems rising out of the assigned reading and the lectures. Here, the student will be given an opportunity to demonstrate not only his knowledge of scholarly method and form but also his capacity for making his own discoveries or establishing relationships that have not already been observed. The writing he will be required to do will give him valuable experience in the discovery of material, the construction of a hypothetical answer to the problem he has set himself, and the effective presentation of the judiciously weighed evidence for and against his hypothesis.

The seminars that the graduate student takes will differ from his courses in the intensity with which the subject is studied; here the graduate teacher will almost certainly be a specialist, and the student will be expected to conduct himself as a potential specialist. In this situation, he will probably become conscious of a more strenuous competitiveness among his peers than he has encountered even in his graduate courses. The seminar will give him a chance not only to increase his knowledge of the aspect of the field being investigated but also to test the strength and depth of his own interest in it. The graduate teacher of a seminar may indeed regard it as an opportunity to discover promising scholarly disciples whose dissertations he will supervise and whose later careers he may interest himself in promoting.

The graduate student will not be long in discovering that one of the most important requirements he will have to meet is the passing of a general examination on the field that he has chosen to study. The earlier practice of graduate schools was to combine the examination of the field and the defense of the dissertation in one exhausting three-hour oral examination set after the dissertation has been accepted and approved. Now it is fairly general practice to separate these two examinations and to require the passing of the general examination in the field before the student is allowed to embark on the production of a dissertation. Such a general examination, which is sometimes written and sometimes oral and sometimes a combination of written and oral, is usually planned to come at the end of the first two years of graduate study, and the courses the student takes during those years are intended, in a sense, to prepare him for the examination. But his courses will not by themselves prepare him adequately for this examination. He will discover that he will have time to take all too few courses to acquaint him satisfactorily with the range of his subject, and he will have to plan to do a good deal of reading, aside from his reading for courses, to fill in the gaps of his knowledge. For such reading, he will have to find a sufficient, if not really an adequate, amount of time, and he will be fortunate if, during his undergraduate years, he has already developed the habit of reading widely in the field that he ultimately decides to make his own.

In all probability, the graduate student will have decided on the field out of which his dissertation will develop, before he passes the general examination, but it is not likely that he will win approval of his subject until after the examination. The choice of both the dissertation subject and the faculty member who is to supervise the dissertation is crucial in the matter of satisfying this all-important requirement for the Doctor's degree. The dissertation subject should be chosen only after the most careful thought and with the best available advice. On the one hand, the subject should not be so large that it would take years of research to deal with it adequately; on the other hand, it should not be so small that the results of a thorough investigation of it would be picayune. It should not be overambitious; it should not, on the other hand, reduce itself to an obvious matter of assembling material. The most important consideration is its practicability, the probability that the dissertation can be completed satisfactorily within a year of research and writing. Three years are as much as the acquisition of a Doctor's degree deserves. But hundreds of graduate students have discovered that they are devoting considerably more than three years to their training, simply because they have undertaken the production of a dissertation that could not possibly be completed in a year freed completely for it.

Though the choice of a supervisor for one's dissertation is not so crucial as the choice of a subject, it is important. The major consideration is whether or not the master and the disciple can work happily together; a comfortable and easy relationship between the two is far more important than the amount of time and thought that enters into their cooperation. In some cases, where the graduate student has demonstrated that he can work independently, the amount of co-operation during the process of research may be very slight. In other cases, the personalities of the two concerned may make advisable a fairly close and continuous cooperation.

The graduate student will make a profound mistake if he labors under the illusion that his dissertation is going to be of world-shaking importance or that he is turning out a really distinguished book. He is neither old enough nor mature enough to produce a book that will compare favorably with the best productions of experienced and accomplished scholars. He will be well advised if he regards his dissertation as an attempt to demonstrate that he can successfully maintain a research project of considerable size and that he has acquired what he is supposed to acquire—the training that will ultimately make him a genuine productive scholar. While he will be fortunate if he can persuade himself that his dissertation is worth the time and thought and energy and money he is devoting to it, he should guard himself against being victimized by illusions as to the transcendent importance of either his subject or of himself as an investigator of his subject. He will be wisest if he sees his dissertation as an extensive exercise in the methods of research.

Holders of the Doctor's degree are notorious for their failure to become productive scholars. A very large proportion of American Doctors of Philosophy never publish anything except their dissertations. In other words, hundreds of graduate students who have been trained to become scholars are content with being teachers. The implications of this unquestioned fact are clear. Most graduate students struggle to get a Doctor's degree not because they are interested in becoming scholars but because they know it is advisable for them to hold the academic union card if they are to ascend the academic ladder rapidly. It has frequently been suggested that graduate schools should develop programs leading to two distinct degrees, one emphasizing preparation for teaching and the other preparation for scholarship.

Even teachers who do not, regretfully or happily, become productive scholars may have gained from their graduate-school experience a knowledge of materials and methods, a conception of the meaning (and the limitations) of the scientific approach to the humanities and the social sciences, a respect for fact, the habit of viewing with suspicion what poses as fact, and a capacity for distinguishing between what is and what is not evidence. If these are the only abiding results of three years of graduate study, one might maintain that they are so fundamental to intellectual integrity that they will heighten the quality of the teaching to which most Ph.D.'s will be content to devote themselves.

5

Academic Arenas

Persons only slightly acquainted with higher education in America are likely to be unaware of the great diversity of institutions in which professors may initiate and pursue their careers. In England and in Europe, *university* is the generic term for institutions of higher education; in America, for historic reasons, *college* is the loose term that the man in the street uses without realizing the multiplicity of types of institutions that it embraces. The young person who is considering college teaching as a profession cannot content himself with this vague and careless usage; it behooves him to become aware of the very considerable variety of institutions in which he may envisage a potential career for himself.

It might be well to start with the most characteristic American institution of higher education, the liberal arts college, of which there are actually hundreds scattered across the United States. The liberal arts college, as its name suggests, is not a professional or a technical school; it is an institution that is primarily devoted to giving its students a liberal—as distinct from a professional or technical—education. Since the meaning of liberal education shifts from one historical period to another, since its meaning is still a subject of constant debate by college presidents, faculties, and educators generally, and since even an attempt to define it would involve the writing

of a book much longer than this one, I shall content myself
with saying flatly that the purpose of a liberal education is the
introduction of the student to the fields of knowledge that
have traditionally constituted the subject matter considered
appropriate to a nonprofessional education: literature and the
fine arts, philosophy and religion, the social sciences, and the
natural sciences. The objective of this introduction is the
development of an individual who will be reasonably well
informed about the traditional knowledge connected with
these fields and who, as a result of his contact with them and
knowledge of them, will be able to live a richer and more
meaningful life than if he had been denied contact with them.
Liberal education, essentially, has no utility; it does not teach
a man how to earn a living; it attempts to teach him how he
may live more abundantly, in mind, body, and spirit. Secondarily, to be sure, the training the student gets in college
may serve, more or less directly, as a foundation for the professional training he pursues in a graduate school of arts and
sciences or in such a professional school as a law school, a
medical school, a theological seminary, or a school of business administration. The college, then, has a dual function,
but it will be faithless to its primary objective if it allows itself to emphasize preprofessional training at the expense of
the general culture of its students.

The values that are common to all liberally pursued studies
are the reduction of ignorance, the increase of information,
the minimizing of prejudice and the enhancement of tolerance,
training in distinguishing between what is and is not a fact,
training in the technique for discovering the whereabouts of
facts, a respect for logic, and devotion to its application to
areas to which it is pertinent and a rejection of it in areas
where it is not pertinent, an awareness of the past and of its
influence on the present, a comprehension of the character
of contemporary society, a conception of the complexity of

the world in which we live and of the human beings and institutions in that world.

The number of subjects that are deemed necessary for or appropriate to a liberal education has increased tremendously in the last century or so. If you were to look at a century-old catalogue of a liberal arts college, you would find that the curriculum consisted of Greek and Latin, mathematics, philosophy, natural philosophy (that is, the sciences), rhetoric, and probably Christian theology. The curriculum of a contemporary liberal arts college would probably include art, astronomy, biology, chemistry, economics, English, French, geology, German, government (or political science), history, Latin, mathematics, music, philosophy, physical education, physics, psychology, religion, sociology, and Spanish. Such a curriculum becomes more intelligible and meaningful when one realizes that these subjects fall into four main classes: literature and the arts, philosophy and religion, the social sciences, and the natural—that is, the biological and physical—sciences.

The liberal arts college may be distinguished from the university by its restriction or practical restriction to undergraduate instruction in the subjects listed above. Characteristically, the number of its faculty and students is small, as compared to even the small university. It is also distinguished by the fact that normally it has no professional or technical school immediately associated with it. But in a period of rapidly expanding education like the present and the immediate future, it would be hazardous to define smallness by a specific figure. Traditionally, however, the liberal arts college has usually been thought of as small so long as its undergraduates did not number more than a thousand and its faculty not more than a hundred, but such figures will rapidly become as obsolete as last year's tax rate.

Liberal arts colleges may be classified as denominational

and nondenominational, coeducational and noncoeducational. Many of the older liberal arts colleges in the United States were founded by one or another of the Protestant sects, primarily, for the training of students who might go into the ministry and, secondly, for the strengthening of the faith of the students already belonging to the sect. Many of these colleges have loosened or severed their denominational connection and have passed out of the control of a governing body representative of the sect. There still exist, however, a considerable number of colleges that have not ended their denominational connection, and these colleges rightly expect that their faculty and students will conform to or at least not attack the doctrines and the ethical codes prescribed by the sect. Most small liberal arts colleges, however, affirm their Christian heritage more or less vigorously by holding religious services on Sunday and sometimes during the week, although admission to none of them involves adherence to any religious faith, Christian or non-Christian. The rapidly growing number of Roman Catholic colleges usually admit Protestants.

Most liberal arts colleges nowadays are coeducational, although some of these attempt to maintain what they regard as a satisfactory proportion between men and women students. Along the Eastern seaboard and occasionally in the Midwest and Far West, however, there are liberal arts colleges that are still noncoeducational. Liberal arts colleges to which admission is restricted to men or women have behind them an educational tradition that goes back to the Middle Ages. The mediaeval monasteries and nunneries set a pattern for the segregation of the sexes, and the ancient universities of Oxford and Cambridge followed the pattern. The segregation of young males in liberal arts colleges in America was a natural consequence of this tradition in a day long before the movement for the emancipation of women brought about the founding of similar institutions for women.

The college teacher, in embarking on and pursuing his career, may find himself confronted by a choice between a coeducational and a noncoeducational institution. If he is fortunate in his institutional connections, he may, in the course of his teaching career, have the opportunity to teach classes of men, classes of women, and mixed classes. He will discover considerable differences in the atmospheres that invest classes of these three types. He may feel that in a class made up only of men the atmosphere is somewhat more relaxed and free than in that of a class of women students and that his men students are less docile and perhaps more challenging than women students might be. On the other hand, in classes restricted to women he may feel that his students work harder but accept his views less critically than his men students. If, however, there is a happy balance between the sexes, he may find the juxtaposition of masculine and feminine views challenging; he may indeed discover that it is possible to play on and exploit these differences effectively and meaningfully.

Characteristically, the small liberal arts college in America was founded in or near a small town, and sometimes it has come to dominate the community of which it was initially a minor part. Characteristically, also, these colleges were frequently established in places that were not too easy of access on the ground, apparently, that it was a good idea to preserve the students from the contamination traditional romanticism associated with urban life. There are still small colleges that are remote from the highways of American life, although they are daily becoming more and more accessible.

At its best, the life of a small liberal arts college can be very delightful and engaging. Its comparative isolation and its relative smallness make possible the development of a considerable sense of community between members of the faculty and the student body. Every member of the faculty will know—at least slightly—every other member of the faculty and will be aware of his interests and attitudes. If the morale of the institution is good—and the morale depends ultimately on the relations between the president and the faculty—the sense of cohesiveness and of devotion to common objectives may make for a genuine feeling of "belonging." If the student body remains relatively small, those of the faculty who are interested will know, even though not intimately, most of the student body, and members of the student body who are socially conscious will have a fairly wide acquaintance among students and members of the faculty. A college is no longer small, is indeed beginning to move into the large category when the members of the faculty no longer feel that they can get to know each other and when members of the student body are no longer able to recognize other members of their student generation.

Delightful as the life of a small college may be, its smallness may result in certain disadvantages that an ambitious and exacting college teacher may find disturbing or irksome. In the first place a small college in a small community is like a goldfish bowl. There is no—or almost no—privacy: all one's actions are visible to all the other members of the community, and academic curiosity is lively and academic eyesight good. One lives one's private life in public; one's domestic affairs become a community concern. In the second place the self-sufficient and independent character of the small college, its isolation from the great world, its tendency to become ingrown and to choose too many of its faculty from among its own alumni may discourage the degree of self-criticism that would prevent the development of self-satisfaction and smugness. Furthermore, since in the small college the emphasis is likely to be on teaching, although lip service may be paid to the importance of research, there may be no pressure from the community and little individual incentive to do anything except teach; the result may be that the less ambitious or lazier members of the faculty may cease growing intellectually and may content themselves with an amount of information and knowledge quite sufficient to satisfy the not excessive demands of their undergraduate audiences. Finally, life in a small college may be so agreeable and unexacting that members of the faculty may be reluctant to leave—even if they have an opportunity to do so—and meet the challenge of a new and more demanding environment. Staying on year after year in a small college may result in one's digging his academic ruts deeper and deeper until the human vehicle almost disappears from view.

The American university may be distinguished from the liberal arts college not only by its size but by its complexity. The college is a comparatively simple social organism; the university is, in various degrees, complex. Normally, the American university may be defined as a sizable liberal arts college around which are grouped a varying number of professional schools. The professional schools most frequently found in an American university are those devoted to medicine, law, theology, business (or business administration), agriculture, and education. Universities may be so small that they will not exceed in numbers some of the larger colleges; they may be so large as to be numerically overpowering. Universities may also be classified as private and public. Most of the older American universities—Harvard, Yale, Princeton, for example—are private universities, that is to say, they operate, not on grants by the state but on the income from endowments accumulated through generation after generation of private contributions, plus the gifts that result from the annual drive for contributions from living alumni, now a not inconsiderable contribution to the income of the private university.

The private university in America manifests advantages that arise from a long tradition and a distinguished history.

There is no question that the older and larger private universities in America have—whether or not they deserve it—a reputation and a prestige that no publicly controlled universities can boast. The private university, moreover, simply by reason of the fact that it is privately and not publicly controlled, is enviably independent of public opinion and social pressures. It is in a position to defend and protect the academic freedom that is indispensable to the satisfactory conduct of intellectual and scientific inquiry.

The American state university, on the other hand, is one of the wonders of the modern educational world. It is a more characteristic expression of the American spirit than even the most distinguished and time-hallowed private university. If it is situated in a wealthy state and if its administration maintains a satisfactory relationship with the legislature that votes its funds, its resulting size and complexity may be amazing. Traditionally, its admissions policy has been more democratic than that of any other type of American institution of higher education. The less distinguished of these institutions may still be required by law to admit the graduates of all the accredited high schools in the state; in practice, however, the better state universities attempt to control the quality of the hordes of students who apply for admission by limiting their acceptance to students who have attained a good average in their high-school work. Even so, the freshman classes at the larger state universities are bound to be extremely large, and the mortality likewise is very considerable. The liberal arts college at a state university is usually more impressive quantitatively than qualitatively. It is common practice in many such institutions to turn over a great deal of the elementary instruction to graduate students who teach part time and study part time. Such an arrangement commends itself to many graduate students who might not be able to pursue their studies with the aim of achieving a Ph.D. if it were not possible to support themselves by part-time teaching. But these graduate students—and *their* students—suffer from the divided loyalty. The former may find themselves devoting themselves to their teaching at the expense of their graduate work or devoting themselves to their graduate work at the expense of their teaching.

The atmosphere of the university, whether private or public, differs from that of the liberal arts college, in the first place, by reason of the size of the institution and, in the second place, by its inevitable juxtaposition of undergraduate and graduate students. The larger and more numerous the graduate schools, the less important, however profitable in terms of income from tuition, the undergraduate body is likely to be. The faculty's lack of serious concern with undergraduates may, on the other hand, be offset by the fact that, for the brighter and more alert undergraduates, the graduate student, if known personally, may serve as a stimulus and, more significantly, as a symbol of a more advanced stage of the students' formal education. It would not be difficult to demonstrate that the presence of graduate students in considerable numbers encourages the better and some of the less good undergraduates to go on to graduate study either in their home institution or some similar or superior institution. This process may well be furthered if older members of the faculty actually come into contact with some of the brighter undergraduates in advanced courses that they teach, although the possibility of such encouragement diminishes in proportion to the size of even the advanced courses for undergraduates.

For members of the faculty, life in a large private or public university has a very different tone from that in a small liberal arts college. The size of the faculty and the intensified interest in their special fields of research felt by those members of it who conduct graduate courses in the professional schools discourage the development of contacts between teachers in different disciplines. If one were to observe the behavior patterns at a university's faculty club, he would probably see that most faculty members are in the habit of lunching with other members of their own departments. In a large university, furthermore, the departments themselves are so large that, unless a faculty member is unusually energetic and conscientious socially, he may not know well or even recognize without an effort some of the newer members of his own department! Then, too, unless he is unusually democratic in his associations, he will tend to limit his close acquaintances to those of his own age group or, more significantly, to those of the same academic rank. All department members—at least nowadays—are likely to be very conscious of the psychological, social, and professional chasm that yawns between the tenure group and the nontenure group in a department. The first group has achieved academic "immortality"; the nontenure group hopes for it and yearns for it.

For some faculty members, at least, the large university does have advantages, social and professional, that the small liberal arts college does not offer. Particularly, if the university is in or near a large city, the faculty member may have a degree of privacy, a degree of invisibility that he could never enjoy in a liberal arts college in a small town or city. Most of the faculty of a liberal arts college are likely to live fairly near the college, sometimes in residential "developments" provided or made possible by the college; their domestic habits and customs, their tastes and amusements are bound to be a matter of general knowledge and, consequently, of social approbation or disapprobation. Faculty members of a large university in or near a large city are likely to be widely dispersed residentially and they are, therefore, less open to observation and judgment than the swimmers in the fishbowl of the small college.

Professionally, the teacher in a large university may very

well find the intellectual atmosphere more stimulating than that of the college; the very presence, in and out of one's department, of scholars of nation-wide or world-wide reputation may be a source of inspiration to younger members in the process of shaping and promoting their careers. Furthermore, since the university inevitably puts far more emphasis on research and publication than does the college, its faculty members feel an intellectual, if not a moral, obligation to pursue their research and to produce books and articles which, they hope, will be favorably received. In the university, administration and faculty alike assume that everyone is working on something, aside from his teaching, and, in some universities, periodic checkups are made on the individual's scholarly projects. It should, however, be said that the academic mind is rather easily satisfied if a modest degree of progress can be reported. The university, therefore, offers an atmosphere in which the scholar, the research man, is likely to be happier than the professor who is primarily interested in teaching. If the administration is tolerant and broad-minded, a very good teacher may expect to be rewarded, ultimately if not rapidly, in even a large university; he is, however, likely to develop a more or less successfully repressed sense of intellectual inferiority if he is surrounded by scholars who are devoted to research and who are building up reputations by steady and successful publication.

For the teacher who hopes to achieve fairly close relations with some of his better students, the university is not a very satisfactory academic arena. If he is a popular teacher, his undergraduate classes are almost certain to be too large to permit any personal contact with his students, and, in the larger universities, graduate classes—and even seminars nowadays—are too large to make any very satisfactory personal contacts humanly possible. The professor in a university is likely to get his profoundest satisfactions not only from the results of his own researches but also from his work and his continuing association with the graduate students whose Doctor's theses he directs. If his interest in such students is more than merely advisory, he will come to regard them, after they have taken their degrees, as his disciples, and will, both before and after his retirement, do whatever he can to advance their academic careers. But, increasingly and unfortunately, the number of graduate students whose theses distinguished professors find themselves directing is becoming so large that even here little personal contact and association are possible. The production of Doctor's theses is coming to be more and more an assembly-line operation.

At the opposite end of the academic scale from the large university is the junior college. In the history of the evolution of American higher education, the junior college is a comparatively recent type of emerging academic organism. In 1920 there were only 53 junior colleges in the United States, with a student enrollment of something over 8,000. Only a decade later, there were 277, with an enrollment of more than 55,000 students. By the mid-century, the number had risen to almost 500, with more than a quarter of a million students enrolled. By 1957 the number had increased to 667. In the future the junior college will certainly play an even more conspicuous role than it has played in the recent past. Already, particularly in the spectacularly developing civilization of California, the junior college is multiplying rapidly, and the increase in other parts of the country is bound to accelerate. This striking increase is a direct response to the demands of high-school graduates who want to continue their education but who, for one or another reason, cannot attend a four-year college or university. Even in prosperous America, the families of an increasing number of high-school graduates cannot possibly afford to send their children to a four-year college or university. The junior college, which is usually a nonresidential institution, can, therefore, provide a relatively inexpensive mode of continuing the student's education for at least two years. Another reason for the increased attendance at junior colleges is intellectual. There are many students who wish to enter upon at least the earlier stages of higher education but who would find it difficult, in the face of increasingly intense competition for entrance into college, to gain admittance to a four-year institution. And yet the social pressure to engage in at least a modest amount of higher education is so tremendous that the junior college is almost the most striking feature of our current educational landscape.

The purpose of the junior college is to offer college courses of freshman and sophomore grade to its students. Students may receive an Associate of Arts degree on the successful completion of their work. In addition to the academic program, junior colleges may also provide some advanced instruction in the various vocational studies already initiated in high school. In terms of corporate responsibility, junior colleges are of several varieties. Some, particularly in the eastern part of the country, are private institutions. A very much larger number are supported by municipalities. Others, especially in the West, are state supported and may, indeed, be administrative sections of the state university although their locale may be very remote from the parent university. In the near future the junior college will become a relatively inexpensive means of providing at least two years of higher education for the hordes of students that the state universities and the private colleges and universities will not be able to accommodate. Probably every junior college aspires to grow up to be a four-year liberal arts college, and it is likely that the strongest of those that are able to win wide community support will develop slowly into such colleges.

To neither the teacher nor the student is the junior college likely to prove the most attractive base for operations. The student who may have built up a glamorous picture of under-graduate life may very well be profoundly disappointed in the failure of the junior college to realize his dream of college life. Its students who live at home will not find going to college substantially or significantly different from going to high school. Most of them will have no chance to profit by the valuable, if trying, experience of living away from home probably for the first time and being, to a degree never before experienced, personally responsible for the way in which they distribute their time among their studies and outside activities or between work and idleness.

The teacher at the junior college is likely to be somewhat disconcerted by the uneven intellectual quality of his students. Some of these students may not have done sufficiently good work to lay a satisfactory foundation for classes of college quality. Many of the students, moreover, will appropriately be considering their education in the junior college as terminal and will not be very much interested in pursuing their studies with sufficient seriousness to prepare for later work in a college or university to which they might transfer. On the other hand, since in the next few decades the standards of admission to liberal arts college and universities are bound to rise steadily, and since only top-flight students are likely to be accepted, the intellectual quality of the junior college student bodies will be considerably improved by the inclusion of promising or excellent students who, for one or another reason, are unable to continue their studies elsewhere. The teacher, if he is intellectually exacting and ambitious, may not find his colleagues as stimulating as university colleagues might be. Since many of them will not anticipate continuing their graduate studies until they have secured their Doctor's degree, they will hardly stimulate their ambitious young colleague to devote himself to further study and research if he has already acquired the Doctor's degree himself.

The observations just made of the junior college as an academic arena probably hold true of most teachers colleges and, therefore, need not be elaborated. The teachers college —as the name suggests—is an institution designed for the training of teachers, primarily for service in the secondary schools. The older teachers colleges have frequently grown out of what used to be called Normal Schools; they have become four-year colleges and have taken on some of the features of liberal arts colleges in order to gain a more professional status. Characteristic of the teachers colleges is an emphasis not on liberal education for its own sake but on education as professional preparation for a career in secondary-school teaching; the emphasis is utilitarian and functional and not so disinterested and genuinely liberal as college education at least aims to be. Since the major function of the teachers college is the training of teachers, the emphasis is not so much on deepening the student's understanding of such subjects as English, history, or physics as it is on training him in the most effective techniques for teaching such subjects in the classroom. To put it even more simply, the concern is not with *what* to teach but with *how* to teach. Critics of the teachers colleges are inclined to maintain that their concern is not with content nor with the research that might enrich and illuminate some content but with method. In so far as teaching is a science, however, there is every reason to believe that neophytes may learn a great deal that is fundamental and useful about the teaching process from professional courses in pedagogy. Certainly, the assumption of most graduate schools that the possession of a Doctor's degree is a sufficient and adequate preparation for college teaching is belied by the floundering of Ph.D. novices, a process that ends only when, by wasteful trial and error, they hit upon a method of teaching that is appropriate to their type of personality. To the extent that teaching is an art, it cannot be taught directly. The art of teaching is acquired by observation and imitation of good teachers and also by the slow and painful discovery of the devices a teacher with a particular personality finds effective in his relations with students in the mass or as individuals.

In the early history of institutes of technology in this country, the humanities and the social sciences played minor roles, but more recently their administrators have come to believe that scientists and engineers will be better scientists and engineers if they have been brought into contact with other than professional subjects. Accordingly, in the better institutes of technology, such as the Massachusetts Institute of Technology, the California Institute of Technology, and the Carnegie Institute of Technology, there has been an increase in the emphasis on the humanities and the social sciences, and their abundant resources have made it possible for them to attract first-rate teachers and give them a greater freedom than they would find in liberal arts colleges to plan their programs and to conduct their courses as seems wisest in view of the special nature of their student clientele. Despite the favorable aspects of teaching in an institute of technology for the teacher of the humanities or the social scientist, there is the unquestioned disadvantage that he is living in an atmosphere that is essentially alien to his professional concern; he may come to feel, quite naturally, that his subject seems decidedly secondary in importance to those of his technical colleagues; unless he is resourceful in keeping up his contacts with other workers in his field, he may cut himself off from them and the possible stimulation they might give him. Since what he is doing is only supplementary to the main objectives of his colleagues and students, he may feel little incentive himself, unless he is unusually independent, self-sufficient, and self-propelling, to keep on with his own studies and to grow in depth and breadth and understanding through continuous devotion to his own research and publication. On the other hand, for the professor who is content to be a teacher and perhaps some of those who hope to play successfully the roles of teacher and scholar, his contacts with students in an institute of technology can be very rewarding. In the first place, he can count on a very high level of intelligence in his student clientele, since at least the better institutes of technology can be highly selective in their admissions policy, and, in the second place, he can have the satisfaction of discovering that these good young minds, if properly appealed to, can be as intelligently responsive to the best he has to offer as the best students in a liberal arts college or university.

I have tried to suggest the natures of the different types of educational institutions in which the person who aspires to be a professor may find himself teaching and some of the advantages and disadvantages of each type of institution. Obviously one type of professor might find himself professionally happy in a type of institution in which another type would be miserable. What is important to note at this point is that there *is* a considerable variety of academic arenas and that it is possible and perhaps desirable that a person bent on academic advancement and recognition should move from one type of institution to another. What it is most important to realize is that in every one of these types of institutions the basically important relation is that between the teacher and the student and that in all of them the devoted teacher may find students who deserve the most intelligent consideration that he can give them and who respond, with gratifying results, to the best that he can offer them in the way of intellectual stimulus and nourishment.

6

The Academic Ladder

Ideally, the aspirant to a professional career should be able to defer his acceptance of a full-time position until he has attained his Doctor's degree. Actually, in all probability, he will find it necessary to seek a full-time teaching position before he has attained his degree. With or without the Doctor's degree, however, he will find himself confronted by the unhappy business of looking for a job. The first step onto the academic ladder is probably the most difficult of all; it is as hazardous and momentous as a child's first step.

The most reputable means of securing one's first academic post is through one's graduate department. The faculty of the graduate school is interested not only in producing good Ph.D.'s but also in placing them advantageously, since the establishment of its Ph.D.'s in reputable and geographically well distributed academic institutions is conducive to building up or maintaining the prestige of the department and is a reliable means of securing a continuing flow of graduate students from the institutions where its products have been placed. In placing its products, the department may act independently or it may cooperate with a placement bureau conducted by the university. If it operates independently, it may turn over the problem of placement to the chairman or his secretary or it may encourage its members to act independently. Through personal or formal contacts with the world of scholarship, the chairman and the senior members of the department may become aware of vacancies in other educational institutions or may indeed be asked to recommend candidates for consideration for such vacancies. The greater the prestige of the department, the more likely it is to be made aware of vacancies for which its products may be recommended. A generation or more ago, the placing of candidates was a very personal and informal procedure. With the increase in the size of graduate schools and the number of educational institutions, job hunting and job procurement have necessitated the development of a more formal and impersonal system. To meet the needs of this complex situation, the university placement bureau has been devised. The bureau acts as an intermediary between the graduate student and the job opportunity. It therefore requires formal registration with it and the preparation of a record of the graduate student's work, along with recommendations from those members of the graduate faculty who are most intimately acquainted with his work. It will be the graduate student's responsibility to see to it that his "papers" are properly and attractively assembled so that they will make as favorable as possible an impression on prospective employers. The securing of impressive recommendations is a matter to which the graduate student should devote whatever tact, shrewdness, and courtesy he can command.

But the graduate student who is seeking an interesting and satisfactory position would do well not to rely exclusively on the services of the university's placement bureau. Another formalized aid to which he should have recourse is the professional association made up of faculty members in his field from all over the country. These professional associations or learned societies, as they are called in academic jargon, only America has developed on an impressive, if not overpowering,

scale. Very early in his graduate-school career, the student
will learn the names and the activities of the learned society
connected with his discipline and the advisability of attending its annual conventions and perhaps joining it as a junior
member. His first experience in attending such a convention
may well be bewildering and awe inspiring. He will discover
that the program of the convention consists of innumerable
concurrent sessions arranged by committees of the association.
Each of these sessions is devoted to the presentation of a number of scholarly papers and a discussion of these papers. On
first attending a learned society's convention, the novice will
probably attend as large a number of sessions as he can schedule and listen attentively to the papers presented. This incred-
ible exhibition of scholarly achievement may stimulate him
if he is self-confident and depress him if he is not sure of his
own powers. Unless his naïveté is excessive, he will not be
slow in discovering that it is much more important to give a
scholarly paper at such a meeting than it is to hear one. He
will also learn that the really good papers presented under
these circumstances will sooner or later appear in one of the
scholarly journals devoted to the publication of research in his
discipline where they can be read and assimilated at leisure.

Even the graduate student who is not in quest of an academic appointment would do well to acquire early the habit
of attending the annual meetings of the professional society
in his field. Indeed, he would do well to join it at the earliest
opportunity, since membership in the association is regarded
by some scholars as an indispensable, though minimal, indication of academic respectability. Attendance at professional
conventions familiarizes the novice with the appearance and
manner and style of the notables in his field; if he listens to
papers he may learn something substantial that he will be
glad to learn; he will get a lively impression of the quality of
the work that is being done by other aspirants for scholarly

distinction; if he is attentive and observant he will learn in which directions the scholarly winds are blowing, what old approaches are falling into desuetude, what new approaches are becoming popular or fashionable. He will learn very soon to pick and choose the papers he is to hear in terms of the quality of the person rather than the subject of the paper. He will observe that only the run-of-the-mill members devote very much time to hearing papers; he may be a little surprised, at first, to observe how much time most members devote to the exchange of academic views and gossip in the always crowded lounges or bars.

If the graduate student attends a meeting of a learned society in the hope of securing an academic post, he should make this his chief business at the convention. Learned societies differ widely in the degree of formality with which their placement service is conducted. In the smaller societies, its operations are entirely informal. They are indeed a face-to-face equivalent of the traditional personal procedure described earlier. The graduate student's patron who becomes informed of the existence of an opening will see to it that his disciple is introduced to the person who is responsible for filling the position and that he has an opportunity to be interviewed by this person. Most learned societies, however, have grown at such an amazing rate that the informal personal procedure is no longer workable. At a convention at which perhaps four thousand members are in attendance, the possibility of making personal contacts diminishes rapidly. Even the elaborate system that is set up for the exchange of personal messages has only hit-or-miss results. Accordingly, more and more vigorous steps are being taken to formalize meetings between persons looking for jobs and persons looking for candidates to fill the jobs. Sometimes, for instance, a particular office is set up where persons in quest of jobs are asked to file their papers; hither, persons in quest of candidates resort, attempt to find papers that suggest interesting candidates, and then leave messages for those whom they wish to interview, indicating the time and place for an interview. At no point in one's academic career does the element of chance play a more decisive role than at the moment when the aspirant gets his first offer. The efficient operation of the system would require the services of a large and experienced secretarial staff, and the setting up of such a staff for a period limited to the three days of the convention would demand a high degree of organizational skill.

In recent years another procedure for securing an initial appointment has become common, at least in disciplines where the number of applicants is extremely large. This procedure is the direct soliciting of positions by means of letters of application. Many graduate students on the verge of taking their Doctor's degrees prepare a form letter expressing their interest in being considered for a possible opening, summarizing their educational experience and the range of their interests, indicating the persons from whom recommendations may be solicited, and sometimes including a formal *curriculum vitae* with a list of publications or prospective publications. This material is then mailed out to the chairmen of departments in institutions where the applicant can imagine himself happily teaching. This method of direct solicitation seems a little immodest. Indeed, I know of only two cases where really good people did secure appointments by the epistolary method, but I have no doubt that it will be resorted to even more frequently in the future than it is at present, since many graduate students prefer writing letters to plunging into the whirlpool of a learned society's convention.

There is a final recourse for the aspirant to a teaching appointment, the professional teachers' agency. A teachers' agency is a business organization that, like any other employment agency, attempts to find jobs for the people who sign up with it. Teachers' agencies, like any other such agencies, are good, bad, and indifferent. They usually operate not only by means of the registration fee paid by applicants but also by the exaction of a certain per cent of the first year's salary of the person for whom they secure a position. In the main, however, I doubt very much whether agencies, unless very astutely managed, are in a position to accumulate information concerning the most promising openings. I have never known any academic administrative officer who resorted to an agency for a list of candidates to be considered, but I probably underestimate the astuteness of the agencies and their usefulness at least to narrowly oriented and informed administrative officers.

Ultimately, of course, an initial appointment to a post is made when an agreement is reached between the administrative representative of an institution or department and the applicant. The former is more likely to be favorably disposed to an applicant if he knows the applicant's recommenders; it is the responsibility of the latter to make himself as attractive as possible, both by letter and in person, to his prospective superior.

The aspirant to a professional career will, I believe, be fortunate if luck or design brings it about that he has a chance to teach in a variety of academic institutions. He should avoid becoming so attached to the first institution to which he is appointed that he comes to feel that he cannot really be happy anywhere else. It is very easy for a young teacher to develop an almost pathological attachment to the first institution to which he is appointed, especially if it is his own alma mater; he does not realize that, despite the differences, one academic institution in America is fundamentally very much like another, that he is likely to find some good students and some congenial faculty members anywhere, and that, in every institution, he will have the opportunity to teach as effectively as he can manage to do. In the preceding chapter, I have attempted to characterize the major types of academic institutions in America; each type has its particular attractions; each has its peculiar disadvantages. Experience in a variety of academic institutions gives the prospective professor a variety of opportunities to develop his interests and gifts. He should, I feel certain, regard appointment to any institution as an opportunity to exploit, legitimately, the chances it offers him to develop his powers in directions that another institution would not offer him. If the prospective professor's activities are not confined to one type of academic arena, his interests will be widened, his personal contacts with faculty and students more various, his knowledge increased, and his competence in the educational process enhanced.

If the graduate student finds it necessary to take a teaching position before he has received his Doctor's degree, he will, in all probability, be made an instructor. If he has already received his degree, he will almost certainly be made an assistant professor. In both cases, the initial contract is not likely to be for more than two years, although it may contain the stipulation that the contract will be renewed if the appointee's work is satisfactory or that he will be promoted when he receives his Doctor's degree. Now, the aspirant to an academic career has his foot on the first or the second rung of the academic ladder. It remains to consider by what means he may make his way to the top rung.

Advancement in an academic career is dependent, of course, on the aspirant's superiors, but the relative importance of his various superiors will depend on the nature and the size of the institution in which he is teaching. In terms of the power structure of the institution, his superiors will be the chairman of his department, the dean of the college or division in which he is teaching, the president of the institution, and the board of trustees that govern the institution. The ultimate powers of appointment, promotion, or dismissal reside in the board of trustees, but, except in a time of crises or a period when the trustees fail to have complete confidence in their president, they take little or no part in the actual decisions as to promotion or dismissal, although legally no appointment, promotion, or dismissal is official until it has been voted by the trustees. The role of the president in these matters varies with the personality of the president and the size of the institution. In a large university, the president is unlikely to take very much personal interest in matters of appointment, promotion, or dismissal, except in the case of really distinguished persons who are being invited to join the faculty or in a case where a member of the faculty has been charged with incompetence or moral turpitude. Concerned as he is with the complex financial problems of a business enterprise like a large university, he is likely to turn over the problems of faculty personnel to the deans of the colleges that constitute the university. In the small liberal arts college, the president, with respect to faculty personnel, will play a role appropriate to his interests and temperament. If the president has no very serious interest in educational policy, he is likely to devote his energies to fund raising, relations with his trustees and alumni, and public relations generally. On the other hand, if the president of a small college has an educational program that he is interested in promoting, he will be intimately concerned with selecting and promoting faculty members who are likely to be sympathetic to his program and useful in carrying it out.

Whatever the official powers of the board of trustees, the president, and the deans may be, the significant decision as to promotion or dismissal is likely to rest with the chairman and the senior members of the department. If the chairman of the department believes in the democratic process, he will see to it that not only his senior colleagues but all the tenure members of the department have a share in arriving at these decisions. He may even arrange to have all the members of the department meet any prospective appointee to it.

Wherever the power of decision lies, the grounds for the decision are fairly constant even though they may be so intangible that it is difficult to define them. The grounds for the decision are usually four: the individual's effectiveness as a teacher, his productiveness as a scholar, his reputation in the field in which he is a specialist, and the personal qualities that seem likely to make him an agreeable member of the department and of the academic community. These criteria differ in the degree of their objectivity and subjectivity; they also differ in the weight that is given them in the complex business of arriving at a decision to promote or to dismiss.

As I have pointed out earlier, the weight given to the individual's effectiveness as a teacher depends on the type of academic institution in which he is serving. For personnel in the humanities and the social sciences in junior colleges, teachers colleges, or even institutes of technology, effectiveness in teaching is likely to be the major ground for promotion, although the qualities of the teacher's personality may also count. The weight given effectiveness in teaching in the liberal arts college varies with the nature of the college. I have heard of liberal arts colleges where this gift counted very heavily and scholarly productivity hardly at all. In most liberal arts colleges, an attempt is made to base recommendations for promotion on both effectiveness in teaching and scholarly productivity. Actually, in most cases, the attention to scholarly productivity is a matter of form rather than a matter of fact; it is a kind of lip service that the liberal arts college pays to scholarship. The small liberal arts college gives relatively little weight to the individual's reputation as a specialist.

In the matter of promotion or dismissal, the qualities of the teacher's personality are likely to be given a great deal of weight. After all, the small liberal arts college is a community where everyone knows everyone else and where personal contacts with other members of the faculty are unavoidable. The aspirant's manners, tastes, and general conduct in social relations, therefore, may play a subtle and elusive but decisive role. If he is overaggressive or overassertive, if he is unskillful in concealing his disapprobation of or contempt for some of his colleagues, he is not likely to be regarded as a person who fits easily into the college community. I have heard one aspirant for promotion criticized because other members of the faculty did not find him intellectually stimulating. I must say that I never assumed that it was one of my responsibilities to stimulate my colleagues; if I succeeded in stimulating a few of my students I felt that I had done my duty. From these considerations, it follows that the promotion or dismissal of a younger member of the faculty in a small liberal arts college is a complex and delicate business; it is not surprising that the turnover in such a college is sometimes horrendously large.

A weighty additional reason for the large turnover is the fact that, under the influence of the American Association of University Professors, most reputable colleges have adopted a policy of arriving at a final decision not later than seven years after the beginning of the individual's teaching career. Promotion to an associate professorship almost always carries with it the important fringe benefit of tenure. From the point of view of both the college and the teacher, the momentous decision is whether or not a man is to be elevated to the associate professorship and thus be made a permanent member of the faculty. This policy, which, in academic jargon, is called the "Up or Out" policy, was designed by the AAUP to prevent an institution's keeping men on indefinitely at the lower ranks. It has turned out to be the inevitable cause of a great deal of anxiety and tension among younger members of the faculty, and its result is, as I have suggested, a sometimes spectacular turnover at a fairly advanced stage of the academic career.

The attitude of the academic profession toward tenure has changed fundamentally in the last fifty years. In earlier days the problem of tenure did not weigh heavily on the young teacher. He seems to have been satisfied to have a contract running for two or three years and he felt no doubt that, if he were reasonably successful as a teacher, the contract would be renewed for a similar or even a longer period. He expected that, in the fullness of time, he would be made an associate professor and that the implication of such a promotion would be his ultimate elevation to a full professorship. Tenure was not a word that came frequently to the lips of either teachers or those with administrative authority. Nowadays, tenure has assumed what strikes me as an undue importance in the minds of younger members of the faculty. The younger members of the faculty are intensely aware of the invisible gap between the tenure members and the nontenure members of the faculty.

The elevation of tenure, a fringe benefit that obtains in very few professions, to a position of great psychological importance is not easy to explain. Aside from the "Up or Out" policy, another possible reason is the general drive in American society for security, and this drive in turn may possibly be traced to the traumatic experience that Americans suffered during the Great Depression of the thirties. The drive for security and the overvaluation of tenure probably have neurotic roots as well. If the individual has a sufficient amount of self-confidence, he will not worry excessively about tenure; if he does not get tenure in one institution, he will probably get it in another equally good or better institution.

The elevation of the academic man from an associate professorship to a full professorship is usually an inevitable and painless event, although it is one that may give the individual—but more particularly his wife—a good deal of inner satisfaction. In some cases, however, the recommendation to elevation by those in authority, the president, the dean, the department head, or possibly the body of full professors, may necessitate some formal or informal scrutiny of the achievements of the academic aspirant during the period, whatever it may have been, when he was an associate professor. This, however, is the last occasion, except for the composition of his obituary, when the aspirant's scholarly productivity is likely to be a subject of investigation and evaluation. Since the other criteria for advancement—the aspirant's effectiveness as a teacher, his reputation as a scholar, his congeniality as a member of the academic community—are no longer matters for serious question, the only remaining problem is his productivity. It therefore behooves the aspirant to a full professorship, at least in institutions where the criterion is taken seriously, to organize his personal and professional life during the period of his associate professorship so that he will be able to make significant additions to his list of publications. On this occasion, to be sure, the major scholarly job to which the aspirant has devoted such portion of his academic life as he can salvage for scholarly pursuits will be counted in his favor, even though there have been few objective and tangible results of this great undertaking. A great many associate professors, not to mention even more full professors, have maintained excellent reputations, in and out of their academic communities, by their reiterated announcement of their devotion to a project that some colleague who survives them may be so unfortunate as to be given the responsibility of completing.

Once the aspirant to academic honors has been made a full professor, he may be said to have arrived. There is nothing for him to look forward to except the completion of his major research project, the possible acquisition of an honorary degree from his alma mater or some other friendly institution, and retirement. Neither as an associate professor nor as a full professor can he be deprived of his hard-won distinctions, at least in reputable colleges and universities, except under very unusual circumstances. There are now only two threats, and these not serious, to his sense of security and fulfillment. All reputable institutions subscribe, at least theoretically, to the requirements for dismissal prescribed by the American Association of University Professors. Theoretically, the only just grounds for dismissal are professional incompetence and moral turpitude. A person who has achieved a full professorship need have little fear of dismissal on these grounds. His professional competence should have been firmly established long before he became a full professor. Of moral turpitude, academic communities are far less tolerant. Fortunately, the American academic man, in general, seems to be incredibly well behaved, far better behaved than any other profession except perhaps the clergy. But, if untoward impulses should drive even the full professor into behavior that is strongly disapproved, not so much by the academic community as by the community of which it is a part, the professor's academic career may end with dramatic suddenness.

In the main, however, the state of being a full professor in an American college or university is a singularly blissful state. To be sure, some of his tasks may be tedious, if not boring. As he grows older, he may become increasingly impatient with the reemergence of faculty discussions of time-worn topics of which he has already heard too much. As a more and more influential member of the academic community, he may resent the amount of time that he is called on to devote to administrative duties or committee work. Otherwise, he is singularly free to distribute his energies between the two activities to which he has chosen to devote his life, teaching and research. If he has no interest in producing another scholarly book, article, or review, there is no external compulsion upon him to produce them. If he has lost his initial enthusiasm for teaching, by this time he has learned to teach with a minimum of effort. His reading has been so wide, his knowledge of his subject is so ample that, if his audience is limited to undergraduates, he can draw on the stored riches to carry through any number of class hours. He has read enough professional books; he can put himself to sleep reading detective stories. As Beardsley Ruml observed astutely: "Once permanent tenure is granted, the teacher's relationship to the college community is severed only when he reaches the established age for retirement. His behavior may be irresponsible, offensive, or even wrong as measured by the standards of a community of scholars; but unless he grossly offends the larger community, he is not likely to be disciplined by his faculty peers or by the President and Trustees. In short, individualism is not only condoned by the college community; it is encouraged and protected, because without it the institutional purpose cannot be fully accomplished. Short of gross offense, the restraints upon the individual teacher are chiefly those imposed by his own judgment, self-discipline and integrity." *

In Shakespeare's *As You Like It*, perhaps the most famous speech is the melancholy Jaques' soliloquy on the hallowed topic of the ages of man. Jaques distinguishes seven ages of man and, since seven is a sacred number, it may be pertinent to distinguish seven ages in the career of the professor: college education, graduate school, instructorship, assistant professorship, associate professorship, full professorship, and retirement. Retirement then is, or may be, the crown of the

---

* *Memo to a College Trustee* (New York: McGraw-Hill Book Company, Inc., 1959), pp. 52–53.

professor's life activities: according to the personality and temperament of the professor, it may be either a miserable or a blissful state. If he has been a 100 per cent academic man, he may experience a considerable wrench with the cessation of his professional activities. If he has never identified himself completely with the role of the academic man, he may find retirement a profoundly satisfactory reward for his years of strenuous educational activity. Negatively, he may feel a great sense of relief that he is free from the less attractive responsibilities of the professional life: the paper and examination grading; the more or less compulsory attendance at department meetings, committee meetings, faculty meetings; the tedious rituals of matriculation exercises and commencement exercises; the responsibility for being a productive scholar. Positively, he may be delighted to find himself free for the first time in his life to do the things that he really wants to do. He will, of course, find this condition delightful only if there are activities—aside from formal academic activities—in which he really takes pleasure. If he is a scholar, he is now free to devote himself wholly to his research projects without the distracting obligation to teach. If he is not a scholar, he may now find time to travel to see parts of the world that he has never seen. At least, he will now have time to write whatever it seems to him to be worth writing, simply because it is of interest and importance to him. At last he can read something that he is not bound to read because he has promised to review it or because he has to teach it the next day. Unlike the seventh age, as Jaques describes it, "sans teeth, sans eyes, sans taste, sans everything," retirement may be the most delightful of all the ages in a professor's life.

7

The Professor's Job

Although the professor's major job is commonly assumed to be teaching, it is not easy to define exactly what teaching is. Certainly the teaching process ranges from the most elementary to the most complex and subtle forms of instruction. At its most elementary but also basic and fundamental, teaching is the communication of facts and the ensuring that these facts have been grasped and, within limits, perhaps retained. In the teaching of any subject, it is obviously important that the student should acquire control over the basic facts without which no significant intellectual operation can be undertaken. In this respect, therefore, the professor aims at persuading, encouraging, or insisting that his students acquire by practice and repetition a persistent command of these facts. Since the acquisition or nonacquisition of facts can easily be checked by one or another type of examination, this elementary part of the teacher's job is perhaps the most obvious and demonstrable, if not the most inspiring. But whether the facts concern the conjugation of a French verb, the evidence for the date of a Shakespearean play, the meaning of a term in philosophy, economics, or government, or the reasons for the founding of the Thirteen Colonies, it is one of the professor's major responsibilities to see to it that the students grasp and possess the essential information.

A more subtle, significant, and challenging part of the teaching process is training the student to distinguish between truth and error. This task obviously calls on powers that neither teacher nor student has utilized in the acquisition of basic facts. It involves the capacity for distinguishing between what is and what is not a fact; it involves the weighing of evidence for and against the truth of an alleged fact. If the determination of the fact necessitates the collection and scrutiny of a considerable body of evidence, weighing the evidence becomes a more and more sophisticated intellectual procedure. First of all, the task demands the development in the student of a healthy skepticism with respect to what appear to be facts. Most of the students who enter college assume that whatever they see in print is true, especially if the print appears in a textbook sanctioned by the teacher. In this respect, the beginning—if not the end—of wisdom is the arousing in the student's mind of a thoroughgoing skepticism as to the dependability of the printed page as a source of fact and truth. The development of his education in this area will involve his realization that alleged facts must be checked and rechecked with the most reliable authorities in the field to which the fact is relevant.

The professor is concerned not only with the student's acquisition of facts and the development of his capacity to distinguish between what is and what is not a fact but also with instructing the student in the ways in which he can discover the essential and reliable facts concerning the subject that is being taught. He will not consider that he has trained his students properly until he has accustomed them to using intelligently and speedily the immense resources that it is the function of the college or university library to accumulate and make available to students. The holdings of any college or university library have been classified and arranged so as to make them easily available to the questing student, but if his experience has been limited—as is usually the case—to school or public libraries, he will need a fairly intensive and systematic initiation into the ways and means of finding as quickly as possible the materials relevant to the question he is attempting to answer. He must learn to discover not only the best books dealing with the subject of his investigation but also the technique for exploring the wealth of material buried in important periodicals that will give him the latest evidence concerning the question he is investigating and the latest answers to it.

It is an all-important responsibility of the professor, furthermore, to train his students in the most effective ways of handling and presenting the material that they have discovered. The young student may very well be skilled and devoted in his collection of material but comparatively unskilled in the manipulation of it once it has been collected. This process requires discrimination between what is important and what is not important in the material he has assembled more or less systematically. It also raises immediately the problem of how it is to be organized so as to make a coherent and logical presentation of the portion that is really relevant to the subject of investigation. Finally, it is the professor's unavoidable responsibility to train his students in the use of effective words, correct grammar, and coherent paragraphs. Since one of the marks of the liberally educated person is the ability to write correctly and effectively, every professor —and not merely the one who teaches English composition— should make himself responsible for doing whatever he can to raise the level of correctness and effectiveness in student writing. This is a responsibility that will weigh more and more heavily on all faculties of higher institutions of learning. As both public and private schools become more congested, the amount of training in writing that the heavily burdened teacher is able to give his students will probably shrink almost to the point of invisibility. Even now, a great many students are permitted to enter college or universities who, despite the considerable number of years during which they have spoken and written English, still have very bad writing habits, habits that are apparent not only in errors in grammar and stylistic crudity but in gross errors in spelling and punctuation. Since writing is a habit that has been acquired during the student's childhood and youth, bad habits in writing can not be turned into good habits overnight. What the professor has to do by whatever means he can devise is to encourage his students to substitute good habits for bad habits. His efforts, however, will have little effect, unless he can persuade the student that it is important for him to develop good habits of writing. The student will not be persuaded of the importance of this acquisition unless all the professors with whom he comes in contact agree in regarding the acquisition as one of the most important achievements in college education. Altogether too many professors in departments other than English are content to leave this task to their English colleagues and to work off their annoyance at bad student writing by complaining that the English Department is not doing its job properly. But learning to write correctly and effectively is not a simple matter of taking a course in English composition. Writing is, or should be, one of the major modes by which the student is to be educated; he will find himself writing papers and examinations in every well conducted course that he takes, and the attempt to raise the standard of his written expression and encouragement and insistence that he do so should be a portion of the job of everyone who is teaching in a higher institution of learning.

But none of these responsibilities of the professor can be discharged effectively unless he has the capacity to arouse the student until he feels that what he is doing is worth doing and that he can be interested and excited in doing it. The indispensable prerequisite for this situation is that the professor himself be interested and excited by what he is doing. If he is just going through the motions of teaching while his mind is on something that he considers more important, if he is giving a course so mechanically that he seems to be talking in his sleep, there is little chance that his students will take fire from his performance. It is not inevitable—as the experienced teacher knows very well—that *all* his students will experience the contagion of his excitement; in almost any class of any size, there will be students who have an inordinate capacity for being uninterested and bored by what is going on in the classroom, but the successful teacher will develop a variety of devices to arouse and stimulate and provoke at least the more amenable members of his audience. He will have to discover what methods are congenial to him and what methods have the greatest effect on a particular class or a particular type of student. But more important than devices and methods is the professor's own deep concern with and inexhaustible enthusiasm for what he is teaching; so long as he is possessed of this enthusiasm, some of it will wear off on his students.

In the professor's relations with his students, the establishment of a proper tone is a very important consideration. Of the wrong tones, that of the dogmatic authoritarian is probably the most damaging to the educational process. The dogmatic authoritarian negates the very essence of the pursuit of wisdom. He is so intellectually arrogant that he assumes that his is the final word on the questions on which he is passing judgment; he lacks completely the humility that acknowledges one's personal limitations and the difficulty of arriving at anything like ultimate and unquestionable truth in any area of human experience. His conception of pedagogical success is the students' uncomprehending and parrot-like repetition of the wisdom that he has revealed to them. The martinet is only slightly less reprehensible than the authoritarian. For neurotic reasons of which he himself is probably quite unconscious but of which one is probably a profound psychological insecurity, he turns the classroom into a drill field and enjoys the maintenance of order and conformity for their own sake and not for their possible contribution to the education of his victims. On the other hand, the person who cannot maintain a reasonable degree of order in the classroom and cannot command the respect of his students is likely to be the least effective of all teachers, since the authoritarian and the martinet can at least ensure the acquisition of the rudiments of education as the person with no authority is unable to do. In all honesty, however, it must be said that American college students in the classroom are not only amazingly well behaved but also long suffering, and they have been known to put up with, if not to profit by, their compulsory association with very faulty professorial types.

The professor will win the respect of his students and inspire them to courteous behavior if he himself is worthy of respect and if he treats his students with the courtesy that they deserve. He wins their respect by the seriousness with which he takes his work and by his obvious effort to be as intelligent about it as it is possible for him to be. The American college student is not impressed by the advanced degrees the professor may have earned or been awarded; he is not impressed by—even if he has heard of—the number of his scholarly or unscholarly publications; he *is* impressed by what the professor does in the classroom, the fairness of his treatment of students, his humility before the great works and thinkers he is discussing, the pains he takes to make clear to students what he is teaching and what he expects them to do.

In the professor's relations with his students, he is, I believe, most successful when he assumes the role of a fellow worker who has more years and experience than his younger associates in the classroom but who is generously appreciative of their contributions to the common quest and aware that in many cases his young associates may be even more intelligent than he, if not quite so experienced. It is in some such relationship that the student will realize that education is not rote-like memorization or parrot-like repetition or the acquisition of final answers to problems to which there are no final answers, but the development of the student's latent powers and the bringing of those powers to bear on the immense cultural heritage of the race of men. In this respect, the ideal professor is an elder whose role it is to initiate his young charges into the mystery rites of our complex culture and to prepare them for the responsibilities of intellectual maturity.

The college professor, in the course of his experience, will find himself confronted by a variety of teaching situations that will demand from him rather different responses and techniques. In all probability, he will be called on to lecture to sizable student audiences, to conduct large and small classes, to lead discussion groups, to direct seminars, and to guide the work of a single tutee or a group of tutees.

The academic lecture has an ancient, if not an honorable, ancestry; indeed it was almost the only teaching technique practiced in the mediaeval university, when textbooks were almost nonexistent and other books were so few and expensive as to be possessed only by the wealthy or by ecclesiastical or educational foundations. In the Middle Ages, therefore, the lecture served both as text and as interpretation and comment on the text. The persistence of the lecture as a mode of teaching in a period when all students in the class own or have access to the essential textbooks is an example of the tendency of education to cling to traditional methods. Whether or not the academic lecture that was indispensable in mediaeval times is a mode of teaching suitable to modern education is a question that cannot be answered simply. In the modern world, the most defensible function of the lecture in the areas of the humanities and the social sciences is its use as a means of synthesizing a mass of facts and ideas that it would be impossible for the student, at least in the early stages of his education, to master for himself, since he would not have the capacity to discriminate between what was relevant and what was irrelevant, sound or unsound, and to organize what was worth organizing. The lecture, then, offers the attentive student a convenient short cut to a body of material that it would otherwise be difficult or impossible for him to come by. If the professor is a good lecturer, the lecture may be a means of interesting and exciting students who would be indifferent to what they might find for themselves in textbooks, reserved books, and reference material.

The lecture, however, makes a strong appeal to some of the least admirable characteristics of both the teacher and the student. Once the professor has prepared a lecture and either outlined it or reduced it to writing, he may very well be tempted to regard the subject of the lecture as settled and to have recourse to his outline or his text whenever the time for the lecture's reappearance in the course comes around. The legends concerning dog-eared professorial lecture notes, punctuated suitably, if ineffectively, with academic jokes, are not entirely the products of the lively imaginations of students. On the other hand, the student taking notes on a lecture is usually in a state of almost complete passivity; his lecture notes at best are likely to be a travesty of the professor's discourse; at their worst, they may consist of jottings of the professor's wisecracks, adorned with Rorschach-like doodlings, or serious misrepresentations of what the professor was attempting to say. No professor has escaped the embarrassment of discovering on examination papers gross perversions of the truths he had hoped to communicate.

Although I believe that the lecture is for both the teacher and the student the least demanding mode of teaching, that it is, indeed, anachronistic, there is every reason for thinking that it is a method that is going to continue not only to be practiced but to be practiced more and more widely if not more effectively. The lecture is the least expensive device available for mass education; and since it is obvious that in the near future student bodies are going to grow spectacularly, this growth is going to result in larger and larger classes, and the most obvious means of teaching these classes will be to lecture to them. Not only are more and more professors going to be called on to lecture, but they are going to find themselves asked to resort to the now available mechanical means for broadcasting lectures. Even prosperous universities are finding it difficult to provide lecture rooms large enough to accommodate hundreds of students, and overflow classes will probably not see the speaker but will listen to his voice transmitted by a public-address system. There will also be increased use of televised lectures, and students may become accustomed to the screen personalities of their professors and rarely, if ever, see them in person.

In any case, the aspiring professor would do well to realize that he should develop sufficient artistry on the lecture platform to prevent his finding lecturing painful or terrifying. A successful and effective professorial lecturer needs to call to his assistance some of the arts of the actor on the one hand and of the clergyman on the other. He must learn to use his voice so effectively as to avoid monotony of delivery and to give variety of tone and emphasis to what he is saying. He must learn to use his body appropriately; he should have, in other words, a good stage presence; he should be able to give the impression that he is perfectly at ease in the presence of his audience. He should learn to use gestures to give variety to his appearance and to emphasize what he wants to make impressive. He should cultivate clarity of diction and take particular pains to be clear and exact when giving references that students are intended to consult or directions for their assignments and tasks. Blackboard and chalk are his obvious stage properties and, with training and experience, they can be used to add a visual dimension to the lecture and to serve as additional means of clarification. Like the clergyman as well as the actor, the professor should hope to move and stir the students' feelings not only to sustain their interest but also to involve them sufficiently in what is being said so that they will not remain indifferent but react either positively or negatively. He must hope to inspire his students, to arouse in them a curiosity about the subject of discourse that will carry beyond the classroom and will move them to pursue independently their investigation of the subject.

In classes that number from a hundred to five hundred (or even more), the professor will certainly feel that the lecture is the only possible method of teaching, but even here he will be well advised to try to establish a more intimate contact with the class by asking occasional questions to encourage his students to feel that they are not merely passive and uncritical takers of notes but individuals and intelligences with whom he is really concerned. He will be fortunate if it is the practice of his department to supplement lectures by meetings with small sections of the class, meetings that will be devoted to discussing the subject of the lecture and the reading assigned in connection with it.

The conduct of a discussion group requires very different powers and skills from those involved in giving an effective and telling lecture. If the meeting of the group is not to take on the elementary character of a recitation in which the

teacher merely checks to see whether or not the students
have read the assignments or understood the purport of the
lecture, the professor must try to develop the power to stimulate the critical faculties of his students; he must attempt to
start genuine discussions not merely between himself and the
students but among the members of the class. The aim here
is to avoid the discussion's deteriorating into a mere setting
forth of the students' unreasoned prejudices and to encourage
the students' support of their views by the most substantial
evidence, the most logical arguments that they can command.
The professor should attempt to involve as large a number
of the group as possible in the discussion. At its best, the discussion should call out spontaneous contributions from all or
nearly all the members of the group; at its worst, the professor
should feel free to exert some pressure on the less verbally
forward and the less contentious members of the group. In
every such group there are bound to be a few rather ob-
streperously vociferous individuals; in order to prevent their
getting into the spotlight and staying there, the professor
should devise means of restraining them tactfully so that the
less expressive students will not develop a feeling of resent-
ment toward their talkative companions and lapse into a passivity even less productive than that of the takers of lecture
notes.

There are two other teaching situations with which the
professor will probably have to deal: the seminar and the
tutorial. The seminar is made up of a small group of students,
probably not more than ten or a dozen, who are engaged
in more or less independent and intensive studies of the topic
or period that is the subject of the seminar. The function of
the seminar is the training of the student in the elements of
independent investigation. The training usually takes the form
of a report or series of reports in which the student organizes
and presents his findings to the group. The seminar usually

meets not more frequently than once a week, and the sessions run to two hours and a half or three hours. Since the student is working independently and since the investigation involves a good deal of outside reading and note taking, one of the problems confronting the director of the seminar is the use he will make of the meetings before the students are ready to present their reports for criticism and discussion. He may decide that it will be wise, after he has defined the area of investigation, and assigned the topic of individual projects, not to have meetings of the group until the reports are ready for presentation but to meet his students individually for advice and consultation concerning their projects. What the director of a seminar must attempt to avoid is carrying most of the burden of the group meeting himself and turning the sessions into miniature lectures. For various reasons he may conclude that it will be preferable to have his students work on a number of small projects and to arrange for frequent sessions at which their reports may be given. On the occasions of these reports, the director should bring about a significant interaction among the members of the group by requiring one or preferably two members to act as critics of the report that is being presented. Such a procedure will produce the best results if the student critics have an opportunity to study the report and prepare comments on it before the session of the seminar. It may prove advisable to require the student to prepare an original and two carbon copies of his report so that both the professor and the student critics may study it before it is presented. It may require a considerable amount of ingenuity on the part of the director to involve others than the student critics in comments on the report, but he may very well feel free to call on the other members to express their informal views of the report immediately after it has been presented and before the student critics speak. The teacher's contribution to the education of the students in the seminar will consist of the advice and direction he can give them as to sources of valuable material and methods of organizing and presenting the material, comments on the manner in which the report was presented, that is, the student's effectiveness in reading the report that he has written, and—unquestionably— a thorough, painstaking written criticism of the student's final production. Any student may very well feel aggrieved if a paper to which he devoted hours and hours of preparation is returned to him with brief and perfunctory comments on the substance, structure, or style of his report. Detailed and searching comments on seminar papers are the most effective means of bringing home to advanced students the importance of writing correctly, clearly, and effectively, the indispensability of fidelity to good form in the supporting material in footnotes and bibliography, and judiciousness and logical soundness in the presentation of evidence relevant to the thesis.

The tutorial is the most intimate mode of teaching in vogue in American higher institutions of learning. It consists in the professor's meeting certainly with not more than five students, for the discussion of previously assigned reading. Here, the college teacher has the best possible opportunity to become acquainted with the personalities and the intelligences of his students. Here, he can use to the best advantage whatever skills he has to encourage students to express themselves correctly and intelligently, to probe below the surfaces of the texts being discussed, and to bring to bear upon the texts whatever he can summon from his wider reading and experience to illuminate them. For teachers adept in bringing students out and contriving interplay between their reactions, the tutorial is perhaps the most attractive and effective of available modes of teaching.

A variation on the tutorial just described is the individual tutorial, the purpose of which is the direction of an individual research project that may lead to the student's winning honors in the departments in which he is working. Here, the personality of the professor and the personality of the student may determine the number and nature of their contacts. If the professor is persuaded that the student is mature enough to work regularly and consecutively by himself, he may meet the student only occasionally for advice, consultation, and checking up on the rate of progress that is being maintained. The majority of honor students, however, are likely to need more frequent attention. If they are not checked up on regularly, they may allow their obligations to daily assignments and short-range projects to take precedence over their long-term project and find, toward the end of the college year, that they do not have time left to complete their research project satisfactorily. If the tutor meets with each of his tutees for an hour once a week, he will serve, in a manner of speaking, as the student's conscience; the meeting itself will be a reminder that it is the student's responsibility to devote a certain amount of time each week to his project and to make a modest degree of progress in the direction of his larger goal. The individual tutorial session itself may be devoted to the student's reporting informally on the progress he has made since the last meeting and to the tutor's suggesting research resources of which the student should take advantage immediately. If the honors project is creative rather than critical, if, in other words, the student has chosen to work for honors by doing imaginative writing or making a series of prints or painting a series of pictures, the tutor will probably find it advisable to keep fairly closely in touch—perhaps in regular weekly sessions—with his tutee. In the case of a tutorial in imaginative writing, weekly sessions will give the tutor the chance to work more closely and critically with the manuscripts submitted than if he were to wait for their deferred completion. This mode of teaching, although it is time-consuming for the tutor and very costly for the institution, may be very rewarding to both teacher and student since it makes it possible for them to get to know each other intimately and to work together constructively toward some goal. The student may very well feel, at the successful conclusion of his project, that carrying it through was one of the most significant educational experiences that college has given him.

If the professor should rise to the height of being a member of the graduate-school faculty of a university, he will find himself in a teaching situation that differs strikingly from any of the others that we are considering. He will find himself giving formal lectures to large classes of advanced undergraduates and graduate students; he will find himself directing seminars in the frontier areas of his special field. Perhaps his most significant work—aside from his own research—will take the form of the direction of Doctoral theses. The method of conducting a seminar we have already considered; the direction of Doctoral theses may very well be regarded as the undergraduate individual tutorial raised to a very much higher power. The Doctoral thesis is, as we have seen, the crowning effort of the period of graduate study; the student may be assumed to be thoroughly informed about the whole range of his field and to have at his command the methods and the techniques of scholarly investigation. By the time he begins work on his thesis, he has decided on a field of investigation and a subject in that field that will, with hard work and luck, result in an acceptable thesis. As in the case of the individual undergraduate tutorial, the number of contacts between the director of the thesis and his disciple will depend on their personalities and the professor's sense of responsibility. If the professor is persuaded that his disciple can be trusted to proceed under his own steam, he may think it safe to leave the student to his own resources and to delay the reading of the thesis until it is almost ready for presentation. The truly responsible professor, however, will realize that his experience has given him resources that he should make available to the student, that he may be able to assist him in avoiding errors and wasting time, and that, therefore, he should see the student with some degree of regularity to check on the rate of progress and the quality of the work being done. Such frequent contacts may be good for the student's morale, since they will allay the notion that he is working in a vacuum into which no air from even the academic world is penetrating. Since the professor is concerned that the thesis should do credit not only to the student but to himself, he will certainly see to it that he renders whatever assistance will enhance the quality of the thesis in terms of its subject matter, the organization of its material, the quality of its stylistic expression, the cogency of the argument, and meticulous documentation with footnotes and bibliography.

If the primary responsibility of the professor is teaching, the second responsibility is research. A great many professors, it must be admitted, believe and act on the belief that research is their primary and teaching their secondary responsibility, but certainly in all the institutions we have considered except the university, teaching should be the main concern of professors in the humanities and the social sciences. There are a number of reasons why research takes precedence over teaching in the minds of university administrators and the heads of graduate departments. The objective of graduate study, as we have seen, is training men to do research and to go on doing research after they are launched on their careers as teachers. University presidents, academic deans, and department heads regard research as important because the publication of scholarly articles and books is a more objective way of measuring academic success than success as a teacher in a classroom. In most institutions it is an unwritten, if an absurd, law that the teacher's classroom is inviolate and that direct personal observation of the teacher's performance is taboo. A violation of this taboo, it is felt, would do subtle damage to the profounder reticences of the academic personality. Estimation of the professor's success as a teacher has to be arrived at, therefore, on the basis of such reports as reach the ears of the persons whose responsibility it is to bring about academic advancement or discouragement. Faculty members even look askance at administrators who make any systematic attempt to collect data from students on their judgments of their teachers. Most professors, therefore, agree that research and the publication of the results of their research are the most reliable evidence of their achievements and the most satisfactory reasons for their advancement up the academic ladder.

The problem of the relative emphasis on teaching and research cannot be settled theoretically; it can be settled only in terms of the individual professor and the type of institution in which he finds himself. The temperaments of professors, if allowed free rein, will determine whether they are to be primarily teachers, or primarily research men, or among the few who can achieve a happy balance between teaching and research. Unfortunately, in some institutions, the temperaments of professors are not given free rein; some institutional administrators and heads of departments make it clear to young men who are added to the faculty that academic advancement depends on scholarly productivity. In this situation, the person who does not take naturally to research may find himself compelled to devote a part of his time and energy to projects in which he is not profoundly interested; the results of such compulsory application to research may win such a person promotion and tenure, but they are not likely to be of first-rate quality. Since, however, the quantity of scholarly publication is a much more objective criterion than its quality, many not too discriminating administrators will content themselves with the number and not the nature of the items in the aspirant's "scholarly" bibliography.

The emphasis on research differs from institution to institution. It is likely to be heaviest in the universities, whether public or private, and in the more distinguished liberal arts colleges; it is likely to be least heavy in junior colleges, teachers colleges, and institutes of technology. Paradoxically, the professor who is temperamentally allergic to research may find himself happiest in an institution of higher education where the chief concern is not with liberal education in its wider sense.

To my mind, the best argument for a professor's giving some attention to research is that it tends to keep his mind alive and growing. If his sole concern is teaching, there is the risk that it may become a matter of mere routine, its inevitable repetitiousness tedious, and his response to it flaccid. If his field of research is really relevant to what he is teaching, his investigations should deepen his understanding of his subject, give him new insights into it, and keep his response to it fresh and eager. There *is* sound ground for maintaining that the professor should have *some* serious professional concern other than teaching. Fortunately, the conception of such concern has widened conspicuously in the modern academic world. If the professor's interests are creative rather than scholarly, if he is a poet, a novelist, a painter, or a musician, then his creative activity has come to be regarded as an acceptable substitute for the research engaged in by his noncreative colleagues. For such creative persons the problem of emphasis takes on a different form. The captive poet or novelist or painter finds himself confronting the problem of the distribution of his time and energy between teaching and creative activity. He runs two risks. He may neglect his creative activity for the sake of his teaching or he may neglect his teaching for the sake of his creative activity. There is a very real risk that his creative impulse, which should be the primary concern of the artist, may suffer or atrophy. The writer in particular may find his creative energy siphoned off in his unconscious participation in the creative efforts of his students. Here, as in the case of teaching versus research, the golden mean is difficult to achieve.

The nature of the professor's research depends obviously on the nature of the field in which he is teaching. In the humanities, the philosopher may find engrossing the study of some major philosophy, a philosophical system, or a basic concept, or he may find it most stimulating to investigate problems in the fields of aesthetics or ethics. The professors of literature, in all probability, will have chosen, as graduate students, the field or period or literary type in which they are going to specialize and they may continue their investigation of this or related fields in the maturity of their careers. The professor of fine arts, similarly, will usually aim at becoming an authority on some period of the history of the fine arts or on some artist who is both historically and aesthetically significant. What is most important is that the professor as a research man should be genuinely interested in what he is studying and believe in its importance and significance.

The professor concerned with research should find the tension between his responsibilities as a teacher and his responsibilities as a scholar considerably mitigated by the amount of free time that it is customary for him to have at his disposal. The long summer vacation is a traditional fringe benefit of a career in higher education; its origins are lost in history, and no one seems to have been moved to raise the question as to whether there is any really logical justification for such extended freedom from teaching. As a matter of fact, there *is* no really good reason why teachers should not teach and students should not study at least eleven months of the year.

The conventional justification of the long summer vacation for college teachers is that it gives them an opportunity to pursue their researches; it is a privilege—as professors are wont to forget—that no other profession enjoys. I, therefore, have little or no sympathy with the perennial complaint of professors that they have insufficient time for research. If they were to put their long summer vacations to effective use, they would have quite time enough to do all the research necessary to preserve their self-respect, to keep their minds alive, to win the approval of their superiors, and to rise in the academic world.

Teaching and research, however, no matter how their claims are adjusted, do not constitute the whole of the professor's job. The professor is a cog in the wheels of the complex organization of a college or university, and, as a cog, he will discover that teaching and research are not the only contributions that he is expected to make to the effective operation of the academic machine. A college or university, like any other institutional organism, has a tendency to multiply functions and to utilize its personnel for the carrying out of its functions. Some of these functions have to do with problems of individual students; others have to do with various phases of the effective operation of the academic organization as a unit. The functions that have to do with the individual student concern his health, his living conditions, his social behavior, and his educational development. The responsibility for his health, the conditions in which he lives, and his behavior in the academic community is usually delegated to deans or assistant deans, who may also be part-time members of the faculty. The general responsibility for his intellectual development rests with the faculty. As more and more students have entered American institutions of higher education, there has been a marked increase in the amount of time and attention given to guidance and counseling. Fifty years ago, the college or university assumed that the student could solve his own problems by self-counseling; nowadays, at least in the smaller colleges, every student is assigned to a faculty member who assists the student in planning his program of studies and who is assumed to be ready to give advice and counsel to the student on any aspect of his college life. Much of this counseling is purely formal and could be done as effectively by an intelligent administrative secretary. Whether or not the counseling becomes something more than a clarification for the student of the college requirements and a checking up to make sure that he is meeting these requirements depends on the unpredictable result of the relationship between the personality of the faculty member and that of the student. Despite the efforts of deans to assign freshmen and sophomore students to sympathetic faculty counselors, the proportion of relationships meaningful and significant to either the faculty member or the student is disappointingly small. Once, however, the student has chosen the field in which he is to do his major work and is assigned or chooses some member of the department for guidance, there is a very much better chance that the relationship will have a significant effect not only on the student's performance in college but possibly on his later career. If the faculty member develops a sincere interest in the student and if the student finds the faculty member sympathetic and admirable, the faculty member may stimulate the student to use his powers to the limit or may even furnish a kind of pattern that the student may attempt to emulate in his own later professional career. This sort of influence, although invaluable, cannot be estimated by any device of objective measurement.

The other obligations of a faculty member rise out of the problems that inevitably face a college or a university as an institution. Some of these problems are educational in the broader sense; others concern the faculty as members of an academic community. There is an ingrained tendency of college and university administrators to turn such problems over to committees made up partly of administrators and partly of faculty members, and, in some institutions, especially the smaller ones, there is constant pressure from the faculty to increase its share of responsibility for discussing such problems and arriving at the best possible solutions of them. Almost no institution is so complacent as to believe that it has arrived at the best possible program of study that it can provide, and it is obviously the responsibility of the faculty, through its curriculum committee, to consider revisions in the curriculum and to recommend them to the administration for implementation. Faculty members also are as concerned as deans with the academic progress of their students or their failure to make academic progress, and almost certainly faculty members on appropriate committees will have some voice in arriving at decisions as to putting students on probation or dismissing them from the institution for failing to meet its requirements. But there are noneducational committees on which faculty members may find themselves spending time that is inevitably taken from that which they might devote to teaching and research. They may serve on committees responsible for the choice of candidates for honorary degrees. They will obviously be more concerned with committees that have to do with some feature of their lives as members of an academic community, with salaries, with housing, and with the fringe benefits that play an increasing part in making one institution more attractive than another. Although academic faculties have never been unionized, they always constitute a more or less solidly organized pressure group whose objective it is to get the most favorable working (or loafing) conditions possible from administrators and trustees. Inevitably, tensions between academic management and academic labor develop, and in these cases faculty members may participate in committee work that makes very heavy demands on their time and energy.

Colleges and universities, like other bureaucracies, as we have said, have a tendency to multiply functions and to create committees to carry out these functions. Recurrently, an attempt will be made to cut down on these structural excrescences, but they have an unhappy faculty for emerging under other forms with new titles. One of the reasons for this recurrent proliferation of committees is that there are faculty members who enjoy committee work and thrive on it. Professors tend to be verbally fixated; some of them are compulsive talkers, and committees provide them with a congenial forum for the expression of their relevant or irrelevant ideas. The work accomplished by most academic committees could be done much more efficiently by competent and trusted administrators, but there is no doubt that the faculty member who enjoys committee work will find in most American colleges or universities more than ample opportunity to satisfy his need for self-expression and argument. He will not be a member of a faculty for very long before he comes to be known as a good committee man, in other words, as a good organization man, and, without any effort on his part, he may find himself serving enthusiastically on several time-consuming and inefficient committees. Not to be a good committee man may win him the unenviable reputation of not being a congenial and cooperative member of the academic community. I do not mean to say that a member of an academic community, like a member of a monastic order, does not have responsibilities. The faculty member who does not give some of his time to considering the problems of the community as a community is practicing a self-indulgent seclusiveness, but, as in the case of the balance between teaching and research, the individual faculty member will have to work out for himself the most satisfactory distribution of his time and energy among teaching, research, and contributions to the solution of the problems of the academic community.

8

Professor's Day

Up to this point, our consideration of the professorial career has been theoretical and abstract. Now it may be well to turn from abstraction to concretion and to try to give an impression of what a particular day in a particular professor's life is like, in other words, to take a cross section of a life and a career for which there has been long preparation and for which there is an indefinite future. Perhaps the reader should be warned that the "hero" of the following narrative is distinctly more restive under his academic obligations and somewhat more critical of some academic practices than the average professor probably is, but it seems advisable to try to give vividness and specificity to the narrative rather than to present the professor as an abstract character in an academic morality play.

Professor Smithers could *not* get to sleep. Once a psychoanalyst had asked him what he thought about before he went to sleep, expecting, he felt sure, some revealing erotic preoccupation. "I always go over the events of the day," he had said, "and plan what I am going to do tomorrow."

"How dull!" the analyst had said.

The professor *had had* a very fatiguing day. He could not but envy his wife, Elizabeth, who, in the twin bed hardly an

122

arm's length away, had already found release from the inevitable distractions of family life and the weariness she must
have felt after her successful but demanding dinner party. It
soothed him slightly to think how beautiful she was, even in
sleep, and how fortunate it was that she had kept her looks
despite the wear and tear of bringing four children into the
world and assuming the responsibility for converting noisy
little animals into presentable human beings. His thoughts
turned to Betty Gamble, the wife of the assistant professor
whom they had entertained at dinner. Young as she was and
superficially attractive, she showed signs of turning into one
of those dominating academic dowagers who made his nerve
ends tingle with apprehension. How on earth had young
Gamble, who seemed the shy, sensitive type, happened to
pick her? The answer probably was that she had picked him,
and, once she fastened on him, there was no getting away. . . .

He must get away from wakefulness into sleep; he had not
had adequate time to prepare for tomorrow's lecture and he
hoped he would be in sufficiently good shape, fluent and resourceful enough, to compensate for his lack of careful
preparation. Today's classes had gone very well, after the
minor crisis at the breakfast table. Elizabeth had organized
the children's early-morning activities so as not to interfere
with his: the scrupulously careful shave so that his dark beard
would not develop five o'clock shadow, the hot shower followed by a cold shower, which he counted on to give him a
sufficient feeling of well-being to make his first class a pleasure
and not an inescapable duty. Before going down to the breakfast nook, he had felt euphoric enough to give particular attention to selecting a tie that would contrast attractively with
his only slightly rumpled gray flannel trousers and dark tweed
jacket. But, prepared as he was to meet his first class, he was
not in the mood to put up with the squabble that had broken
out at the breakfast table. Why couldn't children come into

the world, like Pallas Athena from the brain of Zeus, full-grown, responsible, and possibly wise? If only his children did not have to pass through all those dreadful stages of which Elizabeth had informed herself by consulting the best Yale Guides. "Four is a dreadful age," she would say when David had been unduly destructive, even for a healthy young male. "He'll be better next year. He's behaving just as he is supposed to behave. You wouldn't want your child to be abnormal, would you?" Just the same, he had been vaguely irritated when he kissed her goodbye and started to walk across the campus to his nine o'clock class.

He made a point of greeting appropriately all the students he passed, even when he did not know their names. It was a "tradition" at Belmont that everyone on the campus, faculty and students, knew everyone else, and, to maintain the tradition, everyone except a few curmudgeons on the faculty and a few shy students complied without effort. He felt that these early-morning greetings were particularly important to set the tone of the day. He did not, he confessed, exactly like to have students whom he knew well greet him with an offhand "Hi." After all, he *was* a full professor. Hadn't he a sufficiently dignified appearance to warrant a slightly more formal salutation? Was his own classroom manner too informal? He always addressed his freshmen as Mr., although, when he knew the first names of his juniors and seniors, he used them.

By the time he had reached Chapin Hall, where all his formal classes met, he had recovered his equanimity and was looking forward to meeting his class in freshman English. He liked teaching freshmen, and he approved thoroughly of the departmental policy of including freshman English, not only on the schedules of the unfortunate instructors, who sometimes had two sections, but also on those of the tenure members of the department. He enjoyed all his classes, but a freshman class had a quality that he felt in none of his other classes.

He knew the impression they gave of dewy innocence was sheer illusion; some of them had probably had more experience of corruption than he had had. But, whatever their experience, they were capable of responding to what they read with a spontaneity and frankness that the more cagey upperclassmen had lost or had learned to inhibit. Some of them were still excited about being in college; some of them had not yet come to the conclusion that what went on on the athletic field or in the fraternity house was far more important than anything that could possibly happen in the classroom. He had looked forward particularly to this class because he was returning a bunch of themes that he had finished grading at midnight the night before, and he knew that the class was always a little keyed up at the prospect of getting their themes back, seeing the grades, and reading the extensive comments he had typed on the covers of the themes. Theme reading, Heaven knows, was one of the crosses that teachers of English had to bear all their long lives, and yet, perversely, he enjoyed it. He enjoyed it because it gave him a sense of intimate communication with the minds of these amateur writers that he felt he could achieve by no other means. And yet, he had never organized his time and energy well enough to finish reading a bunch of themes until the very night before the day on which he had promised to return them. Elizabeth, he knew, resented slightly the time he spent reading themes, especially in the evening when, after the children had finally been stored away, she hoped they might relax and gossip or talk over their family problems. But she had almost resigned herself to solitude on the one evening a week before his freshmen themes were due to be returned.

This set had been particularly interesting to read. The class, along with the other sections of the course, had been discussing two autobiographical novels, Dickens' *David Copperfield* and Joyce's *Portrait of the Artist as a Young Man*. One

of the bright young men in the department had thought up
this juxtaposition, and at first he had thought it farfetched.
But he had always found it challenging to make what he could
out of material that at first seemed unpromising, and he and
the class had enjoyed contrasting the techniques in the novels
and discussing the various psychological and social forces that
operated in the maturation of the heroes' personalities. Since
he believed that the reading and the writing in the freshman
course should be integrated, he always tried to devise topics
that would tie the two activities together. He congratulated
himself, a little effusively, over the ingenuity of this assignment: the writing of three incidents, each of which would be
in a style, as in Joyce, appropriate to the age of the single central figure. The results, on the whole, had been so satisfactory
as to be diverting, and he loved to be diverted.

The class had gone very well. As he had entered the classroom and had taken the neat bunch of themes out of his brief
case, a little wave of anticipation had swept over the class, and
they had settled back expectantly to listen to the themes he
had chosen to read. He always tried to plan an interesting program of theme reading, but he sometimes discovered that
what interested him did not interest at least the more burly
members of the class. They found pretentious what he found
rather subtle, for a freshman. This time, however, his selection
had pleased them, probably because the heroes of most of the
incidents were the writers themselves. Accordingly, as he
began reading each paper, the more curious and alert members of the class began looking around at their companions to
see if they could spot the telltale signs of embarrassment on
the face of the writer whose effusion was being submitted
for their comments. In a couple of cases, however, members
of the all-male class had chosen to make the central figure of
their incidents a girl and not a boy, and he had been rather
surprised at the skill displayed in the imaginative identifica-

tion. He might, he felt, with some justice, encourage these young hopefuls to try to write some stories for the manuscript-starved undergraduate literary magazine.

What had emerged in the course of the readings and comments was the rather surprising fact that the freshmen had been more successful in writing in a style appropriate to children and to boys than to young men of their own age. Almost uniformly, in the final episode—and the writers apparently could not bring themselves to feel an imaginative interest in anyone older than themselves—the dialogue became unnatural and stilted, and the verisimilitude characteristic of the earlier episodes disappeared.

He threw the problem out to the class. Why did they, in general, find it difficult to write dialogue that would come naturally from their contemporaries? The responses ranged from the obtuse to the acute. Some of the class insisted that the samples he had given sounded all right to them, that that was the way students talked when they were by themselves. This notion brought a hearty laugh from the more knowing members of the class, and there flashed through his mind memories of the broad, not to say coarse, tone of fraternity-house bull sessions in which he, as an undergraduate, had participated. Others had suggested that it was easier to observe characters at some distance from the writer. One needed perspective, one needed "distantiation" for accurate observation and notation. The discussion went admirably and he was so engrossed in it that finally a slightly restive student had said, "Sir, the bell has rung."

After class, a few students always lingered to ask him to explain what he had meant by comments that he had attempted to make as lucid as possible. Then, he had put his books and the papers belonging to absent students into his brief case and had walked over to the Commons, greeting faculty and students whom he passed. He had had sufficient influence with the departmental chairman, Professor Brink, to get his classes at what he considered the only civilized morning hours at which to teach, nine and eleven. There were hardy souls, he knew, who enjoyed the self-punishment implied in eight o'clock classes; as for himself, he did not feel that he could possibly put on the face you assume to meet the faces that you meet until nine o'clock at least, and barely then. Other members of the faculty, also, contrived to keep the ten o'clock hour free from classes in order to get a coffee break; he preferred to use the vacant hour, an hour in which he hoped no student would violate the silence of his office, to put the final touches on his eleven o'clock lecture, and today, Heaven knows, he needed the whole hour, since his theme reading the night before had left him only a few moments to look over his old notes. But, he realized, he must not carry his antisocial impulses too far; he had better drop in at the Commons and stay the length of at least one cup of coffee.

In the Grill, he avoided the round table where the more highly verbal and extravagantly socialized members of the social science departments usually gathered, and looked around for someone sitting at a smaller table whom he might join. Ah, there was one of their instructors whom this might be a favorable occasion to cultivate, since, sooner or later, he would have to participate in deciding whether the young man was someone whom they wanted to "keep." Pat Wood seemed to be an agreeable young man, well mannered—he had been a Princeton undergraduate and was now working for his Doctor's degree there—serious and very anxious to do the right thing.

"Well, how did it go, Pat?" he asked as he bore his cup of coffee gingerly to the table where the instructor was sitting. So, they had talked about the freshman English course, and the instructor began suggesting delicately ways in which he thought it might be improved. If there was anything that

bored him, it was the perennial discussion of what the freshman English course should be. For him it was a very simple
matter; it was a course in reading and writing, and it did not
seem to him to make very much difference what one read or
wrote; what did make a difference was how much the student
wrote, and he waited for some sign that the young man's appetite for reading freshman themes was not insatiable. He
was cagey, however, and contented himself with suggesting
changes in the reading list. He thought there ought to be more
selections from writers of the Southern Renaissance. (Ah,
that traditional connection between Princeton and the South!)
It seemed time to change the subject, and he thought a little
guiltily of his own neglected research.

"How's the thesis going?"

The young man flinched visibly. He knew that his promotion to an assistant professorship was contingent on the
completion of his dissertation, and the experience of beginning teaching had been so absorbing, if not trying, that he
must admit he had been neglecting his research. But he swal-
lowed manfully and said, "I think it's coming on."

"What is it you're working on? I'm afraid I've forgotten."

"Myth and Symbol in the Poetry of William Butler Yeats.
I'm afraid I haven't done very much on it since I got here, but
I hope to finish it next summer."

He groaned inaudibly. Nowadays, everybody seemed to
be writing dissertations on Yeats or Joyce or James or Melville. The graduate schools had certainly changed since his
time, when no subject that was not straight "scholarship"
would have been countenanced. Probably the change was all
for the good, but it certainly complicated the teaching of
literature. An instructor fresh from the graduate school could
discover more levels of meaning in a novel by Melville or
James than had certainly been dreamed of in their philosophy.

"I know it's tough," he said out of the wisdom of his own

experience. "It's tough to combine teaching and research. But can't you keep a couple of afternoons a week free for it?" And then he remembered seeing young Wood bouncing around on a tennis court. That was where his afternoons went, and in the winter there would be squash. The younger generation was so damned athletic.

"I think I'll manage better next semester when I'm more used to teaching."

"I'm sure you will. . . . Sorry. I've got to look over my notes before eleven o'clock. See you at dinner."

"Yes, thanks."

The notes were a little time-worn, and he could not always be quite sure what bright ideas he had scribbled in the margin, sometimes in not too legible pencil. But he had given the lecture several times before, and, after all, the class had just completed its discussions of the text, *King Lear*, and this was the summarizing lecture. He thought it would go all right; it had before.

The class was a large one. He was, he had to admit, a popular teacher, but he hoped his popularity did not depend entirely on his being an easy, or at least a generous, grader. He liked this class; he liked it because it was large and because it had to meet in a lecture room which gave him a chance to display such platform airs and graces as he had developed in a career in which teaching had been the chief concern. Today what he had been trying to do was to contrast the life views of the characters in the play and to discover what these contrasting views added up to, in terms of *Lebensphilosophie*. There was certainly plenty of evil in the play: evil in nature—the storm on the heath—evil in society, evil in the family—those monstrous daughters, Goneril and Regan—evil in the individual, most subtly in Lear himself. The powers of good were meager in comparison, and, when he had been younger, he had read the play cynically as embodying the triumph of evil. Now it seemed to him that in the play as in life the race was nip and tuck, but that, despite the deaths—the conventional Elizabethan holocaust—of everyone of importance, good had a slight edge. But what interested him even more than the struggle between good and evil and its outcome were the conflicting views of nature, of impersonal and human nature, that the play contained. He felt that, consciously or unconsciously, Shakespeare had assigned the action of the play to a pre-Christian period so that he could feel free to express a wider range of conceptions of nature than a Christian *Weltanschauung* would allow. He, therefore, rejected vigorously attempts that had been made to give the play a definitely Christian coloring; to him, its tone seemed distinctly pagan, and specifically stoic. Ironically, the least sound view of nature, or at least that which seemed least sound to modern man, was put in the mouth of the good man, Gloucester, and the soundest view in that of the most evil man in the play, Edmund. Thus, Gloucester says,

> These late eclipses in the sun and moon portend no good to us. Though the wisdom of nature can reason it thus and thus, yet nature finds itself scourged by the sequent effects. . . . This villain of mine comes under the prediction; there's son against father. The king falls from the bias of nature; there's father against child.

And, immediately after Gloucester's exit, Edmund soliloquizes:

> This is the excellent foppery of the world, that, when we are sick in fortune, (often the surfeit of our own behaviour,) we make guilty of our disasters, the sun, the

moon, and the stars; as if we were villains by necessity; fools, by heavenly compulsion; . . . and all that we are evil in, by a divine thrusting on.

There is a similar range of conceptions of the nature of the gods. Again, Gloucester expresses the most pessimistic view,

> As flies to wanton boys are we to th' gods.
> They kill us for their sport,

and even the faithful Kent asserts

> It is the stars,
> The stars above us, govern our conditions. . . .

On the other hand, after Gloucester's eyes have been put out at Cornwall's order and his servant has dealt him a deadly wound, Albany says,

> This shows you are above,
> You justicers, that these our nether crimes
> So speedily can venge!

But what he hoped to emphasize most were the contrasting attitudes toward suicide, first dramatized in the scene where Edgar thwarts Gloucester's attempt to hurl himself off the cliffs of Dover. More subtly and persuasively later, when Gloucester hears that Lear has been captured by the forces led by his evil daughters, there is the telling interchange of views:

Edgar.   Away, old man; give me thy hand, away!
King Lear has lost, he and his daughter ta'en.
Give me thy hand; come on!

   Gloucester.   No further, sir. A man may rot even here.
   Edgar.   What, in ill thoughts again? *Men must endure*
                  Their going hence, even as their coming
                    hither;
                 Ripeness is all. Come on.
   Gloucester.   And that's true too.

He had timed it nicely; he had finished reading what was perhaps his favorite speech in all Shakespeare just before the bell had rung. He was pleased by the way he had captured and held the attention of the class, although, of course, there was no problem of discipline at Belmont.

He had hoped to be able to go home to lunch, as he always seemed more ready at midday to enjoy the ebullience and vitality of his children than he was on his low-toned mornings. But today he had had to lunch with the senior members of the department. The time had come when they must decide, if possible unanimously, what they were to do about one of their instructors and one of their assistant professors. About Pat Wood, the instructor, the discussion would be amicable; they would, of course, feel that they must talk him over at considerable length, but, even before they began talking, they had almost certainly agreed to recommend the renewal of his contract for two years with the stipulation that he would be elevated to an assistant professorship if and when he completed his dissertation. With respect to Ned Gamble, the assistant professor, there would be more discussion and probably disagreement. Gamble, Smithers felt, was the perfectly conventional product of a perfectly conventional graduate school. He was well trained; he took his work seriously; he had managed to hack a number of articles out of his well conducted but unexciting dissertation on the novels of William Makepeace Thackeray, and he could be counted on to produce an article or two a year; he might even father a book. But Smithers did not find him exactly exciting; if only one could see in him some individual, even if perverse, variation from the academic norm. Smithers was bored by the prospect of the meeting, but he hoped he would not be tempted to alleviate his boredom by playing the devil's advocate.

Professor Brink, the current departmental chairman, had taken the view—perhaps because he was a product of the graduate school that had shaped Ned Gamble so decisively or because he had brought him to the attention of the department originally—that Gamble was a very good man, that he knew, from personal observation—since his office was next to Gamble's—that the boy worked very hard, and that they would be put to it to find anyone in his field as promising as young Gamble seemed to him to be. Professor Francis was inclined to take a somewhat less enthusiastic view. Gamble was a good man, to be sure; he had liked his contributions to the discussion of the sophomore course in English literature, but, personally, he found him somewhat short of brilliant. He could not see him developing into the sort of vigorous individualist one expected a full professor at Belmont to become. Professor Brink demurred gently. Professor Henderson, characteristically and adroitly, sat on the fence; he refrained from taking a position that would annoy his colleague on the right or his colleague on the left or even Assistant Professor Gamble. Smithers felt no compulsion to emphasize his own qualified enthusiasm for his young colleague. Besides, he wanted to avoid self-consciousness when the Gambles came to dinner in the evening. The upshot of the discussion was obvious: Gamble was to be recommended for an associate professorship, including tenure. The chairman, however, felt it necessary to make their action formal.

"Shall I tell the president that we recommend Gamble's promotion unanimously?"

This making light of his judgment, Professor Francis could

hardly countenance. "Well," he said, "I don't know that I can go along with that."

"I'll report your dubieties to the president, then," Brink had said, a little wearily.

"Sorry to break up this happy circle," Smithers said. "I have a tutee coming at one," and he crumpled up his paper napkin, dropped it on the table, and made his escape.

He had looked forward to his weekly session with this tutee, with whom he was to discuss the progress, if any, he was making on his senior thesis. Paul Griffin was the most brilliant student he had had in many years, and he enjoyed his sessions with him. He enjoyed them because he knew that at some point they would clash, and he liked smashing back at Griffin's perverse obstreperousness. They would not come to blows over the work that the boy was supposed to be doing; he was brilliant enough to be allowed to work out his problem in his own subtle way. But Smithers was sure that before the hour was over Griffin's barely concealed contempt for academic life would find an occasion to express itself. It had.

"I know, I know," Smithers had said. "Graduate school does seem to dehydrate some people who go through it."

"If there ever *was* any juice in them," Griffin had observed.

"But it would never desiccate you."

"I doubt if I give it a chance to."

"I hope you will," he said seriously. He could see Griffin as a vital and exciting teacher, a perceptive and subtle critic. He felt certain that the boy had far more promise than he had ever had; he had a more acute and penetrating mind. He could imagine himself, as an old man, taking pride in the fact that this brilliant critic had once been a student of his and that he had done what he could to persuade him to go to graduate school and to become a professor. But, he thought a little sadly, I doubt if he ever will. The idea of talents unused always depressed him.

A knock at the office door had ended their session. "See you next Wednesday," Smithers had said, and Griffin had left. The sight of the student who entered had brought to the boy's mobile mouth the familiar grimace of scorn, his manner of greeting Alan Benson, the young stalwart whose vigorous knock had interrupted them. He had found amusing the involvement of this husky in anything so refined and subtle as the study of English literature. Smithers' welcome, on the contrary, was warm and sincere. As a matter of fact, he found particularly attractive the type of student whom he designated as a "hearty." He liked his vigor; he liked his manliness; bored as he was with exercise and sports, he enjoyed vicariously Benson's agility on the basketball court and the popularity it had won him. But what made it a pleasure to have students like Benson in his advanced courses in literature was the realization that they had sensibilities that it was possible to arouse, that, indeed, they offered perhaps the most conspicuous evidence that Belmont could contribute something significant to a student's education. Benson had told him once that, until the end of his sophomore year, he had never read anything except books about basketball; now he knew not only that the boy read with perceptiveness and intelligence the texts assigned but also was one of the very small number of students who explored the library and bore off books that were opening up a new world to him. Now he wanted help with a term paper he was writing on D. H. Lawrence, and, since Lawrence was one of Smithers' favorites, it was not only easy and pleasant but exciting to call the boy's attention to works of the existence of which he had been unaware. "Come around, and I'll lend you some of my things on Lawrence."

There was another knock at the office door. This time it was Larry Grimes, another case altogether. Grimes, Smithers had discovered by probing delicately to get at the root of the boy's scholastic plight, was suffering from a bad case of a common undergraduate complaint, "father trouble." He had a very successful but dominating father, a father who, apparently, craved the pleasure of building up his own ego through the success of his son. The latter had consistently disappointed him, and the father had not made their relationship easier by comparing the boy unfavorably with his friend next door. Why, Smithers had thought, could not fathers be satisfied with what they had assisted in producing? When Grimes attracted Smithers' attention, he had, he conjectured, been getting back at his father by conscientiously flunking himself out of college. Smithers had sent him to the college psychiatrist, but the boy's resistance to that nervous official was so intense that Smithers had agreed to talk to the boy about his problems whenever the boy felt the need to talk. He was coming on pretty well; by a little administrative sleight-of-hand, Smithers had arranged for him to shift his major from Government to English, and he seemed to be taking hold admirably. He had come in to report his grades for the preceding semester: he had not made the Honor Roll, but, to Smithers' great relief, he was again in good academic standing. If only the boy did not experience an upsurge of the impulse to triumph over his father by disappointing his expectations!

Smithers had hoped that there would be no other visitors during his office hour and, fortunately, there were none. He collected himself and looked a little wearily at the top of his desk. As the college year passed, the piles of unanswered professional letters grew thicker and thicker, in fact, grew so high that they disintegrated in untidy masses around the desk blotter. Among them, he knew there were recommendations he had promised students to write for them. But day after day passed, and the recommendations remained unwritten. When he did get around to writing one, he always tried, without being dishonest, to give the student the benefit of the doubt.

Perhaps in a new job, with new responsibilities, even a student who seemed dull and mediocre might flower unrecognizably. He thought of a shy student who had barely made the grade academically who had returned, a year after graduation, with an almost unrecognizable personality, that of an outgoing and amusingly worldly salesman. He began running through the nearest pile of letters and pulled out a couple of applications for admission to graduate school. If no one else knocked at the door, he might get them written before he had to leave. He turned to his ancient but beloved typewriter, hammered out a recommendation, revised it, copied it as neatly as his eternal amateurishness with the mechanism made possible, and was about to start the second when something made him glance at his watch. It was three o'clock, and he had promised Elizabeth he would be home by three. A little guiltily, he dropped the second recommendation on the most conspicuous pile of unanswered mail, picked up his brief case, locked the door, left the grubby old building where the departmental offices were, and started rapidly across the campus.

It was Wednesday, the day when the Faculty Wives Club met, and Elizabeth, he remembered, had said that she wanted particularly to attend this meeting. Molly Henderson was "giving a paper." At least, it was called "giving a paper"; actually, the "paper" would consist of showing a series of colored slides of scenes in Greece where the Hendersons had spent a year on a Fulbright Exchange Professorship. Elizabeth's appetite for colored slides was not conspicuous, but in the interests of departmental solidarity Elizabeth felt that she must attend and she wanted him to be home to look after David and to welcome the other children when they returned from school.

He had found Elizabeth ready to leave. Smithers had settled down in the most comfortable chair in the living room and luxuriated in the unaccustomed silence of the house. He tried

—but without success—to repress the thought of the committee meeting that he knew that he must attend at four-thirty but that he would have liked to cut. He had hardly had time to light a cigarette—but he must cut down on his smoking. The last yearbook had described him as a chain smoker, and he had not exactly enjoyed its calling the attention of the academic community to even one of his bad habits. Now he heard the soft pat-pat of David's footsteps on the front stairs. Exploratorily, he came into the living room.

"Where's Mama?" he asked a little querulously. He was never in the best of humor when he first woke up.

"Gone to a meeting."

"When will she be back?"

"In time for supper."

"I want a glass of milk." Smithers supplied it and two cookies.

He loved all his children, of course; but David, his last-born, occupied a particularly large niche in his heart. Of course, everybody spoiled him, and he was already showing signs of profiting by their indulgence: he had learned—with extraordinary speed—how to get what he wanted; he had a great deal of charm, and, at four, he knew how to turn it on in a manner that was positively coquettish. He had also learned that, if charm failed him, temper might win the day. When David was thwarted in some injudicious want, he could stage a spectacular tantrum. In any case, Smithers felt certain that David was going to turn out to be the most complex, and therefore the most interesting, of his children.

At this point, Bobbie and Janet had burst into the house like a blast from a hurricane, and the books that Bobbie had dumped on the table in the hallway had promptly crashed to the floor. "Oh, shucks," he said and, scowling, picked them up and made for the refrigerator for his glass of milk.

"Get one for Janet, too, and bring it in here." He wanted

to check up on how things had gone at school today. After all, a good deal was expected of faculty children, not only by their parents but by their teachers. Janet was all right; she wasn't at the head of her class, but she was sufficiently impressed by her status as a faculty child to attempt to do as well as she could. Bobbie was another matter, altogether.

"How did you do today, Bobbie?"

"O.K. Got a sixty in a math test and a ninety on an English theme."

"What was it about?"

"I called it 'My Nymphomaniac Aunt.' The teacher read it to the class and the class howled."

Good God, my sister! Smithers thought. Bobbie, it was plain to see, was going to be a problem. He was far too sophisticated for his years. Where had he picked up such ideas? Certainly not from the conversations in which he and Elizabeth engaged in the presence of the children. At the rate at which Bobbie was progressing in knowledge of the world, what would he be like at twenty? Bored and jaded. *Where* would he be at twenty? That was the practical problem. Bobbie had strongly defined interests: he was passionately interested in books and music; he was passionately uninterested in mathematics and science. Smithers could foresee with painful clarity the sort of record Bobbie would make on his College Aptitude Tests: a high verbal factor and low mathematical factor.

Good old Janet was a different proposition. She wasn't brilliant, but she was dependable. She took after her mother.

"Where's Sukie?" he asked, a little querulously.

"Oh, she's playing with those Fiero kids."

Sukie was painfully democratic, or else she suffered from what the French called *nostalgie de la boue*. The kinds of children she brought home! Sukie certainly brought color into the family life, but sometimes the color did not harmonize very well with the scheme of which he and Elizabeth approved. But she was, he had to admit, an extraordinarily engaging child; you never knew what she was going to say next, but you could be sure it would be something fresh and original, if not a little shocking. Heaven knew what sort of person she would turn out to be, but it would certainly be something interesting, if definitely offbeat.

"Well, David has had his nap. Take him, go find Sukie, and tell her I want her to come home." Janet could be counted on to do what she was asked to do and do it without scowling.

He had looked at his watch. It was four-fifteen. He hoped Elizabeth had not stayed for the "discussion" after the paper or for the gossip session that was formally called tea. No, here she was, just in time.

"Well, how was it?"

"As I expected. Arthur in front of the Acropolis. Molly in front of the Acropolis. Arthur in the Theater of Dionysus. Molly in the Theater of Dionysus in a stance supposed to be Periclean. Oh, it wasn't so bad."

"I have to rush. I've a committee meeting."

"Don't forget we're having the Gambles and Pat Wood for dinner tonight. I'll need you to put the children to bed."

"No, I won't forget." He did not approve of having dinner parties in the middle of the week; they always left him groggy and ill humored the next day. But he *did* see Elizabeth's idea. They had been at Belmont so long that their weekends were always taken up with two or three moves in the intricate game of Faculty Social Life. But Elizabeth, with her strong social sense, was always working up sympathy for the younger members of the faculty and worrying for fear they were not being invited out sufficiently. And the bachelors! She had a perfect passion for mothering bachelors, poor lone wolves, eating in Windsor's dreary Greek restaurants or opening a can of spaghetti in the disorderly kitchenette of a solitary apartment. A midweek dinner party would not prevent their accepting some weekend invitation that they might want to accept. He could see he was in for it; the amount of preparation he would be able to give to his lecture for tomorrow on *Prometheus Unbound* would be minimal, and it was, he thought, as he left the house to cross the campus to the president's office, a difficult play. He ought to reread it, but he was sure he would not have the strength to do so after the party was over. And just where were his notes? If he could not find them, he was sure he could never remember the intricate symbolic pattern he had discovered when he had taught the play two years ago. At the time, he had thought it a quite bright idea and that he might make an article out of it. He sighed. That article had never got itself written, and as for his research . . .

Ideally, he thought, he should have the late afternoon to work on his book. Every full professor at Belmont was supposed to be working on a book, but it was amazing how few of them ever saw the light of day. He had done the conventional things; he had extracted a few articles from his doctor's dissertation and managed to distribute them among a number of fairly reputable scholarly magazines. Five years after he had taken his degree, his university had brought out a considerably revised version of the dissertation and it had had moderately satisfactory reviews, although it had not been hailed as the ground-breaking work that he had felt it was going to be when he was an excited graduate student. But these ritualistic achievements were not enough to satisfy himself or to set a good example to the younger members of the department. This time, he must produce something more original and attention-compelling than his dissertation, which, as he now saw it, had been an extended exercise in research and not a conspicuously original contribution to knowledge.

He thought he had a good idea. He wanted to study the imagery of Shelley with a thoroughness no one else had had the patience to apply to it. It might enhance his reputation, although he felt sure none of his departmental colleagues would have the grace to read it. They might, however, note its publication a little grudgingly.

But the project demanded more time than he ever seemed to be able to find for it. It involved, in the first place, making an infinite number of notes, a card-by-card record of all Shelley's images, and there were a lot of them. He already had two drawers full of three-by-five cards, and he was not more than halfway through the complete poems. In the second place, although he tried to set aside the late afternoon hours for research, something was always turning up that demanded to be done immediately. When, in fact, had he made the last additions to his card file? He felt guilty when he realized that it must have been a month ago.

The clock struck one. He must get to sleep. He got up, tiptoed down the hall to the bathroom, and took two aspirin. Perhaps they would quiet his jangled nerves and let him go to sleep. Perhaps, as the analysts said, reliving the rest of the events of this interminable day would permit him to go to sleep. . . .

Oh, yes, the committee meeting. He knew that it had been an indication of faculty confidence in him that he had been elected to the Advisory Committee and he appreciated this indication of his standing in the academic community, but he deeply resented wasting on college committees the time and energy he should have preferred to devote to his teaching . . . and research.

The ideal form of government for a college community was a benevolent despotism. Let the president and the dean make the decisions, and, if the faculty could not be won over to approve them, throw the rascals out. Belmont's trustees were always acutely conscious of the state of tension or the absence of tension between the administration and the faculty. The president, however, believed profoundly that truth could be arrived at by means of rational discussion, but, as Smithers climbed the steps of the shabby old building that housed the offices of administration, he made up his mind that he at least would not contribute to prolonging the discussion. He felt in the right-hand pocket of his tweed jacket to make sure he had cigarettes enough to alleviate the tension he knew the meeting would induce in him.

What was to be the subject of discussion today? Oh, yes, compulsory chapel. This was a topic that could be counted on to recur at least once in every student generation, and he had heard all the arguments pro and con too many times. The college pastor had maintained that Belmont was, after all, traditionally a Christian college, that it had a responsibility to present the Christian message, and, furthermore, if any further relaxation were made in the very modest requirements for attendance at the Sunday service, they might as well lock up the chapel and he might as well resign. The president had assured him there was no reason for fearing these dire contingencies. They were facing a very subtle problem, but if only they could agree on the fundamental principles underlying the problem, he thought they might get somewhere. Professor Strong (Economics), who, Smithers felt sure, had not set foot in a church since he had happily given away his daughter in marriage, argued that, although Belmont had had a sectarian origin, it was now essentially a secular institution and that, if they were logical, they would recognize its secularity and abolish even the modest requirement as to chapel attendance. "The alumni would not stand for that," the president had interpolated. "They may not have enjoyed chapel any more than they did fraternity initiation, but, since they survived them both, they think that what was good for them is still good for their sons." Professor Black of the Art Department diffidently raised the question as to whether the chapel itself could not be made more appealing aesthetically and—here he was even more diffident—whether the order of service might not be a little more ritualistic. "You know our records show that there are more Episcopalians at Belmont than any other denomination." Professor Black himself was an Episcopalian. Smithers scrunched out a cigarette. "I am not an Episcopalian; in fact, my religious views are probably extremely heterodox. But I should very much regret seeing any softening of the requirement of attendance at chapel. The president is fond of talking about the strong community feeling at Belmont. I know some of my colleagues feel this sense of community in the bleachers at a football game; the only place I get it is in the college chapel."

"Well," the president had finally said, "I think this discussion has been very worth while, even though we have not yet, I think, got down to the basic issues involved. Perhaps, however, we have clarified our own views and are clearer as to each other's views. The special undergraduate committee on compulsory chapel would like to meet with us, and I think we should give them a chance to present their views." We know what *their* views will be without hearing them presented, Smithers thought grimly. "Would you gentlemen be able to meet with them a week from today at four-thirty? I'll be back from my alumni trip by then."

Professor Twitchell of the Biology Department spoke up for the first time. "I had to cut a lab-section to get to today's meeting; I should not like to miss another, next week." On Thursday, Professor Black would be out of town collecting paintings for the next exhibition at the college Art Gallery. Friday was apparently the first free day. The more systematic members of the committee dutifully jotted down "Friday: 4:30 P.M., committee meeting." Smithers felt that he had no reason for jotting it down; he regretted that he would not be able to forget it.

When he reached home again, he heard Elizabeth at work in the kitchen, busy with the complex task of preparing the children's supper and the evening's dinner at once. "Bob," she called, "get the children in, and I'll give them their supper. Be sure they wash their hands." Presently, he had herded the children, all bright and shining, into the breakfast nook.

After their supper, he had guided them upstairs. Elizabeth had established a schedule for their retiring, and tonight, for once, it must be adhered to. There could be no yielding to the inevitable sophistries children employ to postpone the evil hour. David was to go to bed at seven; Sukie at eight; Janet at nine, and Bobbie not later than nine-thirty. Sukie could amuse herself drawing pictures for which she seemed to require an inordinate amount of paper. She had been warned repeatedly, however, not to touch any of the cherished stock on his desk. Janet and Bobbie were supposed to do their homework. David was to go to bed immediately. Smithers undressed him, slipped on his sleeping suit, put him in bed, bent over, and kissed him good night. But he did not like the look in David's eye; he was certain *he* did not regard the day as ended. Presently, he would either call loudly for his mother to come up to kiss him good night or, more probably, he would sidle down the stairs to try out his charms on the unfamiliar guests. But for the moment he was in bed.

In the kitchen, Elizabeth had said: "Bob, will you make the salad dressing? Yours always comes out better than mine, and you might get the cocktail glasses out and the liquor ready." She had made the dessert after the children had left for school in the morning, and Elizabeth was famous for her complicated desserts. The roast was in the oven, the potatoes were baking, the salad was made, and the biscuits were ready to pop in as they had their first cocktails. "I thought we had more gin than this," Smithers had observed as he brandished a half-empty bottle. He liked his Martinis very dry; they induced a beneficent glow that helped him through the evening.

Pat Wood arrived first. By the time the Gambles appeared, Smithers and Pat had already finished their first cocktail. The Gambles' baby sitter, a student who had generally been very prompt, had been late; the coach had kept the team on the field until he had had time only to grab a quick bite in the fraternity-house kitchen. The third cocktails had been a little watery, but he at least—and probably Pat—felt well prepared for the evening by the time they had moved into the dining room.

In fact, the dinner had gone very well. Of course, the meal itself was excellent. Elizabeth could be counted on for that, and during its early stages the effect of the cocktails had persisted sufficiently to make him feel genial, even to Betty Gamble, who sat on his right. "It's such a treat to eat a dinner someone else has slaved over," she had remarked, and he had felt a little guilty that he had resented this interruption of a quiet evening's work. The talk had gone very well, too; it had not, to be sure, been brilliant—he had not expected that —but there had been no awkward silences and no outbreaks of unmannerly disagreements. But the topics that could be counted on to elicit opinion and comment had served admirably: the problem of faculty housing, the low state of public schools that, for economy reasons, most faculty children had to attend, the new members of the faculty, in whom he could work up only a modicum of interest, the amazing skill with which the president's wife sustained a heavy social program with scarcely any help. He had had a moment of discomfort when someone commented on the rapidity with which men in the physical sciences achieved tenure and the academic immortality it implied. He remembered his own reservations about Ned. The effect of three cocktails on Pat

Wood had been noticeable. He had let himself go with a rather surprising frankness and charm. When he got back to his solitary room, he would probably think he had talked too much. Betty had looked at the somewhat brash young man a little critically, and Smithers hoped she would not succeed in turning Ned against him. Betty was obviously used to having the center of the stage, and resented anyone else's grabbing the spotlight.

Mercifully, the party had ended earlier than he had dared hope. After all, as Ned had tactfully observed, they all had classes to meet the next day. A little reluctantly, Pat Wood had refused the proffered nightcap and had trailed along in the wake of the Gambles. Smithers closed the front door and breathed deeply.

"You aren't going to do the dishes tonight," he pleaded.

"Certainly not. I'm going straight to bed."

"I'll be up soon, but I must look over my notes for to-morrow's lecture."

"What's it about?"

"*Prometheus Unbound.*"

"Who unbound him?"

"That's the trouble. I never can remember."

"You will."

He gathered up the cocktail glasses in the living room, and helped Elizabeth clear the dining-room table. The kitchen was a shambles, he thought, as he turned out the lights.

"Good night, dear." Elizabeth paused at the foot of the stairs.

He kissed her good night. "I'll be up soon." He hoped she would be asleep. He was really very tired.

He was still very tired, but not quite so jumpy as when he got to bed. He could feel his mind beginning to drift . . . compulsory chapel . . . the curl of Paul Griffin's lip . . . good old Janet . . . his neglected research. No more of that;

that way madness lay. . . . Ripeness is all, his favorite line in all Shakespeare . . . Elizabeth turned in her sleep . . . sleep . . . sleep . . . sleep . . . sleep.

Professor Smithers, we observe, had had a very full and rather hectic day, although its eventfulness is not seriously exaggerated. Enmeshed as he is in the watches of the night in the infinite details of daily academic and domestic life, he is obviously unable to see the forest for the trees. Confronted, as he might well be, by a direct question as to the satisfactions that the professorial life gave him, he would undoubtedly say that what made its tedious obligations endurable were the never failing stimulus of the companionship of the young, the excitement he almost never failed to derive from the free-ranging activities of the classroom, the faith that he was bringing light and leading to the minds under his care, and the enduring hope that at least some of those under his guidance would develop in their later lives powers that he might possibly envy, and become more astute, productive, and influential as teachers and scholars than he would ever be.

9
Shadows in the Picture

I remember a French critic's remarking that in every good picture there are shadows. My picture of the life of a professor may strike some readers as an unsatisfactory likeness, but at least it is not free from shadows. In other words, the life of a professor is not all sunshine and blue skies; it has its limitations and drawbacks, which it is only fair to point out to the student who is considering college teaching as a profession.

Probably the most obvious shadow in the picture of the professorial life is its relatively modest monetary reward. If one were to estimate the esteem in which the professor is held by American society in terms of the financial recompense that society offers him, one would discover that he is rated slightly higher than a taxi driver and slightly lower than a bricklayer or a skilled mechanic. In most students' eyes, this is the darkest shadow in the picture.

Available figures as to faculty salaries are relatively meaningless, since the over-all averages change from year to year, fortunately in an upward direction, and since there is a wide range in faculty salaries from those paid by a great and wealthy university to those paid by a struggling little sectarian college of liberal arts. But even averages may suggest the generally low financial rewards offered to those who embrace college teaching as a profession. In 1955, the Fund for the Advancement of Education reported the following percentages of persons in various professions earning ten thousand dollars a year or over: physicians and surgeons, 41.0; lawyers, 28.1; dentists, 24.6; architects, 18.1; authors, editors, and reporters, 10.3; college presidents and professors, 5.1. In 1958 the *New York Times* observed editorially: "The salaries of college and university teachers in the United States average $6,120 a year, which is just about what plumbers get in wages." For the years 1959–1960, the American Association of University Professors estimates that the average salaries in the institutions reporting ranged as follows: instructors, $3,450–$6,660; assistant professors, $4,000–$8,750; associate professors, $4,850–$11,750; professors, $5,700–$17,500. Minimum salaries were reported with the following ranges: instructors, $3,250–$6,000; assistant professors, $3,750–$7,750; associate professors, $4,500–$10,000; professors, $5,250–$14,000.

Another shadow in the picture of the college teacher's life is more elusive, and yet it is not unrelated to the low financial rewards of the profession: this is the ambiguous social status of the professor. Since, in America, persons cannot be esteemed or disesteemed in terms of their ancestors or the social class into which they were born, many Americans determine a man's position on the social scale by the size of his income. If a professor seems to be reasonably satisfied to labor for a modest income, there would seem to be no very good reason for looking up to him socially or for placing him very high on the social scale. Such a view contrasts very sharply with the traditional view of the European professor as worthy of respect and deference simply because he *is* a professor.

But the ambiguity of the professor's social status is not due merely to the modest financial returns from teaching. The ordinary American's attitude toward the professor is rather good-naturedly and humorously superior. The sense of superiority has its source in the common notion that the professor is a "queer duck" or an "odd ball." But the absentmindedness of the professor is a stale joke that was more pertinent to the nineteenth than to the twentieth century when academic institutions have taken on the "efficient" character of big business organizations. Since President Franklin D. Roosevelt assembled a Brain Trust of professors to assist him in meeting the problems caused by the Great Depression of the thirties, jokes about the impractical professor have become outmoded, at least in liberal circles, and since physicists have become the high priests of the age of nuclear warfare, there is a danger of professors becoming too practical rather than too impractical. On the other hand, while the nonacademic American feels a certain admiration for a person who devotes himself to intellectual pursuits, he is also vaguely uncomfortable in his presence. I recall a university president's telling me that, if his table companions on an ocean liner asked what his business was, he was going to say that he was a salesman; apparently he felt that the discovery by his nonacademic companions that he was a university president would inhibit easy communication. The professor of English, forced to reveal himself, has all too frequently heard the remark, "Now I shall have to watch my English." Relations between town and gown in a college community are frequently complicated by the town's feeling that the faculty either is in some way superior to it or at least feels itself to be superior to the other citizens in the community.

There is some evidence, to be sure, that the professor is regarded more favorably by nonacademic Americans than he imagines himself to be. Seymour M. Lipset maintains that while the professor "may feel himself neglected and scorned, the community itself places him fairly high when polled on the relative status of occupations. In one such study of ranks of ninety-six occupations, conducted in 1947 by the National

Opinion Research Center of the University of Chicago, college professors rank above every nonpolitical position except that of physicians; artists, musicians in a symphony orchestra, and authors ranked almost as high. Essentially, this study suggests that those in the intellectual occupations enjoy about the same prestige in America as do important businessmen, bankers, and corporation directors" ("American Intellectuals: their Politics and Status," *Daedalus*, Summer 1959, pp. 467–468).

A further complication in the professor's relationship to the society in which he operates is the society's expectation—indeed, insistence—that he shall set a good example in matters of conduct not only to his students but to the community. Just as American society expects the clergyman to exemplify a high ideal of conduct, to furnish an example of good behavior to the laity, so our society expects that the professor shall behave not only decorously but decently. In our society the professor comes close to being regarded as a clergyman who has somehow missed being ordained. Probably the burden of respectability falls more heavily on the secondary-school teacher in a small town, but it cannot be escaped by the person who enters the academic profession.

The burden of respectability varies, to be sure, from institution to institution, from community to community, from one region of the country to another. It probably falls most heavily on the faculty of a small denominational college in the Midwest or the South. There are still institutions that forbid smoking on the campus, and there are still institutions where drinking beer would be regarded as unsuiting a person to a faculty position. Young men in quest of teaching positions would do well to investigate the mores of institutions before they find themselves involved in a situation that would drive them to hypocrisy and duplicity. In a college in a small town or city, the professors and their families live in a social aquarium where their slightest deviation from the mores of the community are immediately apparent. In a city, obviously, the visibility is considerably lessened, and the city itself may permit or at least not censure deviations from the more conventional patterns of behavior.

But there are more serious aspects of behavior that may involve the college professor in difficulties or may indeed bring his career to an abrupt, tragic end. According to the code of the American Association of University Professors, covering tenure, promotion, and dismissal, there are only two grounds on which a professor may legitimately be dropped. One of these is professional incompetence as determined by his faculty peers and not by college presidents or deans; the other is gravely phrased as "moral turpitude." If our society expects the professor's manners to be superior to the nonprofessorial, it certainly expects his morals to be impeccable.

One further element in the relation between the professor and the community needs some attention. He may find himself more or less seriously embroiled with his administration, the trustees of his institution, or the wider community because of the ideas that he entertains and expresses. The dedicated professor leads a life of intellectual exploration and, if he is faithful to his ideal, the pursuit of the truth wherever it may lead and the setting forth of the truth, his discoveries and his utterances may prove very disturbing to persons who are content to live on the vital lies of our civilization. The problem is complicated by the fact that he is at once a member of the academic community, a representative of his institution, an organization man, but also a citizen. As a citizen, he is supposed to have the inalienable right of free speech. As an organization man, he may be made to feel that his utterances should not reflect upon or damage the reputation of the institution that he represents. I read not long ago of a scientist, employed by a great American business organiza-

tion which had a huge contract for defense work, who was
censured for enunciating the obvious truth, "Our missile program is the swan song of a dying civilization." A scientist
on the faculty of an American college or university that was
enjoying government grants for scientific research who made
a similar remark might very well have incurred a similar censure. A government-sponsored academic project the objective of which was the study of the origins of politicians of
minor importance was canceled because the politicians ob-
jected to an investigation of their heritage, training, and attitudes.

A distinction should be made between the professor's utterances that concern the field of his social competence and those
that concern areas that are not relevant to his field. Within
his field, the professor speaks as an authority, and, so long
as he is considered competent and reputable, he should be
allowed to speak his views freely. Outside his field, he is speaking as a citizen and not as a specialist in a discipline. As a
citizen, he should, like any other citizen, enjoy the right of
free speech, whatever it may concern. For this reason, the
American Association of University Professors has always
maintained that a professor is not censurable or dismissable
for entertaining and uttering views that, as an American
citizen, he has every right to hold. Whatever one may think
of the personality or the political views of Henry Wallace,
it was outrageous that professors who openly supported his
campaign for the Presidency should have been dismissed or
even censured. They had as much right as other citizens to
work for or against his election. On the other hand, it is incumbent on a professor, in order to avoid misunderstandings
and difficulties for himself and his institution, to make clear
when, in his public utterances, he is speaking as a professional
and an expert and, therefore, in a sense, as a representative
of his institution, and when he is speaking not as an expert

but as a citizen whose views outside his field are as inexpert and as personal as the next man's.

To most persons in the academic profession, the shadows that I have already filled in will probably seem less dark, less important than those that concern more specifically the activities of the professor as a professor. Of these, the first is the arduousness of the professional preparation requisite to the successful sustaining of a professional career. I have already discussed the nature of the graduate work that he must undertake if he is to acquire the degree of Doctor of Philosophy. In three respects, graduate work may prove burdensome to some students. The first and most obvious is the financial burden. Despite the tremendous amount of money that academic institutions have invested in graduate scholarships and fellowships, and despite the fact that the most brilliant candidates for the Doctor's degree may be able to maintain themselves modestly on a succession of fellowships, the run-of-the-mill graduate student will find that he must somehow finance at least three and probably more years of education following the acquisition of his undergraduate degree.

One currently popular mode of financing graduate work is to acquire a working wife. However, in a prolific period like our own, a wife and children may absorb the graduate student's time and attention and divert his energies from what should be his major concern. Another popular mode of sustaining oneself during the period of graduate study is part-time teaching. Under this system, the graduate student attempts to live a double life, one half of which may seriously interfere with the other. At the best, the combination of part-time teaching and graduate study prolongs the period of quasi-dependency and postpones, sometimes distressingly, the attainment of the coveted degree. On the other hand, systematic and well organized individuals have managed to survive this schizophrenic existence.

Marriage and part-time teaching may intensify the psychological problem that harasses some graduate students at least. For just as the undergraduate is in the rather unhappy state of being neither a boy nor a man, so, the graduate student, unless he is unusually fortunate, is forced to extend his state of dependency into what would normally be independent adult life. Whether the sources of his "income" are his parents, an academic institution, or a foundation, he is not an economically self-sustaining individual; he is not—in the ordinary American sense of the word—working for his living. Whether or not this extension of the period of dependency becomes a psychological problem depends, of course, on the student's temperament, but at any rate, marriage heightens the problem since it involves not one but two or more people in this potentially difficult situation.

It is a common experience for graduates of a small liberal arts college to experience a kind of trauma when they leave the comforting embrace of their alma mater and enter graduate school. In the small college the student will have become accustomed to being treated as an individual, to being known to his professors, to being their personal friend or protégé. He may very frequently have been a little spoiled by a well intentioned but overindulgent alma mater. When he enters a large graduate school—and graduate schools are bound to become more and more densely populated—at least at first he is not regarded as an individual; his teachers are not readily accessible when he wants to consult them or merely to visit with them; and the papers that he has written as well as he could write them are read not by the professor teaching the course but by some perhaps invisible and unreachable instructor. Accustomed to small classes, to seminars limited in number, or individual tutorial sessions, he is now only an anonymity in a large class where the struggle for recognition is more intense than he has ever experienced. It is no wonder, then, that a considerable number of graduate students find the situation so emotionally trying that they give up the struggle at the end of their first year and turn to occupations or professions for which the Doctor's degree is not a prerequisite.

Finally, for some students, graduate study may become an intellectual problem. Even if the graduate student survives the ordeal of the first year, he may find the rest of his graduate-school experience tedious, if not repellent. Here again, the reaction depends on the temperament. If he is a "born scholar," he will perhaps feel that for the first time he has entered an intellectual world in which he is excited and happy. If he is not a "born scholar," he may be alienated by an atmosphere in which no one ever asks whether or not an author or a work is aesthetically good or intellectually worthy. If his interests are "modern," he may feel that the emphasis in the graduate school is anticontemporary. If his natural bent is creative, he is likely to be put off by the essentially scientific and critical atmosphere of the graduate school. He may indeed be torn between the impulse to create and the obligation to desist from creation and devote himself to learning and scholarship. On the other hand, if the student is reasonably adaptable, he may discover that it is possible, indeed somewhat pleasurable, to take on, for the time being, the protective coloration of the research scholar; he may even deceive himself, for a time, into thinking that he is going to devote his life to scholarship.

Even after the aspirant to the college teaching profession has completed his graduate work and mounted one or two steps on the ladder to academic preferment, he may find that the practice of the profession he has chosen is not without its disappointments and annoyances.

One of the first illusions to be shattered is that the life of the professor is comparatively leisurely. A superficial view of the life may conduce to this conclusion. Nonacademic people who have a stirring of curiosity about the professorial life are wont to ask in a tone of unconcealed envy, "How many hours *do* you teach?" and, when the answer is "Nine" or "Twelve" or, at the worst, "Fifteen," they have no difficulty in concluding that the professorial life is pretty soft. They ignore the fact that the time spent in the classroom is a very modest portion of the time the professor devotes to preparing for his appearance in the classroom. It is conventional to assume that students should spend two hours in preparation for every hour they spend in class. The professor may not devote more than two hours to preparation for a particular class meeting, but during these hours he may be synthesizing facts and ideas that he may have devoted months or even years to assembling. Furthermore, the work of the professor—as we have seen—is not confined to meeting classes and preparing for classes. There are also his obligation to be constantly pushing forward with his writing and research and, as he rises on the academic ladder, an increasing burden of extracurricular obligations.

Another of the illusions to be dissipated is that the professor lives so leisurely a life that he has plenty of time to read, especially if he is a teacher of English or one of the modern languages. Nothing could be further from the truth. The college teacher who takes his business seriously is very likely to find, especially as he ascends the academic ladder, that he has practically no time for completely "free" reading. If the college teacher gives the time that he should to the preparation of his classes and to the reading and annotating of student themes and term papers, he will have very little time during the academic year to indulge in "free" reading. Even after he has given a course a modest number of times, he will discover that, if he is to react freshly and suggestively to the literary or nonliterary texts that have been assigned, he must reread the texts and not merely glance over them.

The third illusion that has to be dissipated is the notion that the professor is free to luxuriate in the long summer vacation, a period of release from scheduled work that is longer than that enjoyed by any of the other professions and that constitutes, whatever is done with it, one of the major fringe benefits of the teaching profession. But the serious college teacher or one who is concerned with building a reputation for scholarship soon discovers that the long summer vacation is *not* a vacation but a period when, if he will, he can work uninterruptedly. He is, to be sure, free from his teaching duties, but the time is free for carrying out the pursuits that will enhance his prestige and win him academic recognition. The rationale for the long summer vacation is that it offers the college teacher an opportunity to devote himself to his research without the interruptions of class preparation and classroom duties.

Early in the college teacher's career, rather than later, he is likely to find a more significant occasion for disillusionment in his discovery that the student material with which he is to deal for the rest of his life is not of uniformly high quality. The young teacher, fresh from graduate school, may have been disassociated from his own undergraduate experience sufficiently long to have lost a vivid sense of the very mixed character of the undergraduate student body. In the graduate school, moreover, if he has been fortunate, he may have associated with high-grade minds seriously bent on extending their knowledge and power. Now, he may feel at first disappointed, then irritated, and finally perhaps outraged to discover that his audience does not consist of first-rate or even second-rate intelligences, and that, however fastidious

the admissions policy of an institution may be, many undis-
tinguished intelligences have slipped through the nets.

On an occasion when I found myself protesting the two-
valued orientation that undergraduates use when they classify
their fellows as "good guys" or "drips" or "mooks" or whatever the current pejorative term may be, I took it upon myself to work out my own classification of the undergraduates
I had known over the years in the four institutions of higher
learning in which I had taught. The classification, I am glad
to say, turned out to be ninefold, since nine, like seven, is
a sacred number. I shall give this classification for what it
may be worth: 1. Drips; 2. Thugs; 3. Pseudointellectuals;
4. Anonymities; 5. Solid Citizens; 6. Hearties; 7. Grinds; 8.
Creative Artists and Aesthetes; 9. the Elite.

But undergraduates are not the only persons who cast
shadows on the academic arena. Not all the varieties of the
genus professor are unequivocally attractive. If, on the one
hand, it includes Eager Beavers, Aesthetes, "Born Teachers,"
Scholars, Artists, and the Elite, it also includes Dullards,
Drones, and Organization Men.

The Dullard is perhaps the most trying of professional
types. He is the most trying because he is the last person in
the world to realize that he is dull and he goes about eternally
and happily boring his colleagues and his students. His colleagues are more fortunate than his students, since, except
for his unavoidable presence at department meetings and
faculty meetings, they can escape him if they exercise a little
discretion and ingenuity. His students, on the other hand,
cannot escape him except by cutting classes; for him, the
student audience is veritably the captive audience.

The Drone is considerably less objectionable because his
egocentricity is much less obvious. It is the essence of his
nature to be industrious, and he succeeds in being industrious

by the cultivation of what is ironically called "busy work." As a matter of fact, he is the reverse of the medal of which the shiny side is the Scholar. The Drone is the indefatigable note taker, the accumulator of material, the rapt devotee of projects so insignificant and unilluminating that no one with a sense of humor or sound judgment would waste any time on them. He is so busy accumulating material for scholarly articles that he is not likely to be very productive of publications, and, when he does pull himself together and produce an article, he is lucky if he is able to place it in one of the less distinguished scholarly journals.

The Organization Man is the administrator *manqué*. With luck he would have ceased being a professor and become a dean; with the maximum luck he might have become the hard-working and uninspired president of a small college. He adores committee work and does not resent, indeed relishes, the hours and hours that he can contrive to spend discussing college problems with his unfortunate colleagues. With him, teaching and research are minor considerations, but in them he displays the faculty for devoted and conscientious labor that makes him, in the eyes of the administration, a valuable man to have around.

In the year-in year-out practice of college teaching, there are two further shadows in the picture: the burden of "paper work" and the burden of academic responsibilities that are not directly pedagogical. The aspirant to academic preference who selects English as his teaching field unwittingly condemns himself to a life in which reading students' papers and grading students' examinations are inescapable and onerous chores. He is likely to begin his career with a schedule that consists almost entirely of freshman English sections, and the freshman course, conventionally, is a course in reading and writing. The reading may be agreeable; in fact, astute and democratic chairmen of freshman English courses are well advised when they permit the staff to decide annually on the literary works they are to train their students to read. But, as a service department, the English Department is commonly—if mistakenly—regarded as the one exclusively responsible for the improvement of the student's habits in writing. This burden is indeed a heavy one, since more and more students enter college with little or no experience in writing a composition or theme. Our public schools are now so crowded, classes in them are so unwieldy, teachers are so oppressed with extracurricular activities, social or nonsocial, that there is little wonder that they hesitate to assign writing that would force them to devote exhausting evenings to calling attention to gross grammatical and stylistic errors. Consequently, the job of ridding students of their bad habits and trying to induce them to adopt better ones falls squarely on the shoulders of college English departments. Serious teachers must condition themselves to devote hours and hours to this essentially tedious and uninspiring work. Others who achieve the purer air of the higher ranks of the profession may be freed forever from the obligations of freshman composition, but even they will find that term papers and research papers and hour quizzes and final examinations demand a great deal of attention and require a good deal of their time. No one in the humanities or the social sciences can escape the burden of paper reading completely.

The final shadow in our picture of the professorial life is the pressure of academic responsibilities that are not directly pedagogical but that demand a good deal of time and energy. At the very least, the professor will be expected to attend department meetings with exemplary regularity. He will be fortunate if he belongs to a department in which the meetings are perfunctory or *pro forma*, and the chairman of which, with the assistance of an efficient departmental secretary, deals unobtrusively with all the minutiae involved in the activities of a busy department and does not feel it necessary to report them all to his academic associates. He will be less fortunate if he finds himself in a department the chairman of which not only thinks it his duty to report all the administrative details that he and the secretary have cared for, but also believes that all questions involving the department should be open to full and free discussion.

But department meetings are not the only form of bureaucratic activity in which the professor finds himself involved. Within the department there are meetings of groups responsible for particular courses, and nothing stimulates the urge to argument more than a discussion of texts to be required. Outside the department the dangers multiply. The proliferation of committees is one of the most characteristic features of the academic bureaucracy, and in institutions where the faculty has a measure of control over its operation, good committee men, that is, men who can endure without visible discomfort endless meetings designed to discuss each aspect of the academic community's activities, may expend a great deal of their energy on such meetings.

Finally, there is the faculty meeting which in larger institutions can be safely ignored but which in smaller institutions the faculty is encouraged to think it obligatory to attend. The intelligence displayed by an academic group is in inverse ratio to its size; the larger the group, the lower the level of discussion, for the sizable group has the effect of reducing the intelligence of its members, and professors who are quite intelligent can be incredibly irrelevant and illogical in faculty discussions. Richard Armour, who has obviously had experience in these matters, has put the situation very succinctly and accurately in his poem "Faculty Meeting":

Convened, except for those who make it a point of honor
To be late and thus thought busy,
At four;
Adjourned, after dispatching half an hour's business,
At six.

Scholars, dispassionate and logical in articles for the learned
    journals,
Become passionate and illogical on department budgets,
On promotion and tenure,
And on a change in the wording of section five, paragraph
    three, subparagraph two
Of regulations regarding class attendance;
Patient searchers after truth by means of Bunsen burners,
    microfilms, and the interlibrary loan—
Honest men, modest men, fearless men—open their coats
(Why double-breasted?)
To bare their Phi Beta Kappa keys,
Clear their throats importantly, move, second the motion,
    and, with a faint remembrance of Robert's Rules of Or-
    der,
Call for the question after a furtive glance at their watches.

Faculty members individually
Are people.
Faculty members collectively
Are faculty members.*

This extended consideration of the shadows in the picture
may well prove discouraging to the aspirant for an academic

---

* This poem, first published in *The Pacific Spectator* and reprinted in
"A Professor's Garland of Verses" in *Claremont Quarterly,* is reprinted
here with the gracious permission of the author.

career and academic preferment. It has seemed advisable, however, not to conceal, if not to exaggerate, the shadows in the academic picture, and, after all, the function of shadows in a picture is to emphasize the high lights, which we shall now gladly point out.

10
The Professor's Rewards

Once, after I had given an assembly talk to an audience of undergraduates on the life of a professor and had tried to point out its disadvantages as well as its advantages, the first student who greeted me said, "I was thinking of going into college teaching, but you have pointed out so many disadvantages that I think I have changed my mind." After our perhaps too extended consideration of the shadows in the academic picture, the reader may feel that the high lights we are now to consider do not offer a sufficient contrast to the shadows, but I trust that this will not be the effect of the juxtaposition.

The rewards of college teaching are manifold, but they may perhaps be classified as economic, psychological, social, and intellectual.

I have already said that one of the disadvantages of college teaching as a profession is the comparatively meager financial reward. Actually, this disadvantage may be converted into an advantage by the right-minded professor. The college professor, if he has what I regard as the proper attitude toward the economic aspect of life, has the opportunity to exemplify a way of life that, in Emerson's famous phrase, combines plain living and high thinking. In other words, the professor, like the clergyman, by his way of living may set himself up in opposition to a society in which success is measured by the acquisition of material goods. American society *is* an acquisitive society, but the college professor can distinguish himself from it by living in such a way that he demonstrates his fundamental disagreement with the common measure of success. He has a challenging opportunity to show that one can live decently and productively in a manner that is materially simple and aggressively nonacquisitive. There is no reason, except the frailties common to human nature, including the urge to keep up with the Hinkelfingers, why the college professor should be concerned with the acquisition of material possessions or the maintenance of an upper-middle-class manner of living. In the Middle Ages the potential scholar took vows of poverty before he entered a monastic order to advance his education and practice his profession; and once, in America, persons entering the academic profession took a vow of poverty without realizing it. Now, however, in our affluent society, the college professor may exemplify a way of life that, if moderately ascetic and materially self-denying, is nevertheless rich, socially creative, and determinedly acquisitive of the things of the mind and spirit and heart.

If this self-denying ideal seems too rigorous for the aspirant to the academic life, it should be pointed out in all fairness that there *are* mitigations of the modest financial returns on college teaching. On the merely economic side, there are modest compensations. These compensations take the form of what have come to be called not only in industry but also in academic life "fringe benefits," and in some academic institutions they have become so numerous and so valuable that they give these institutions superior bargaining power in their acquisition and retention of faculty members. The most obvious fringe benefit is the traditional summer vacation, usually three months in length. The professor, to be sure, is not expected to idle away these summer months on the golf course or on a sun-smitten beach. He is expected to improve himself and his possibilities for advancement by means of further study, research, or travel. Many college teachers, it must be confessed, develop a rather remarkable capacity for making what is really self-indulgent idleness pass for absorbing and productive work. Foreign travel in particular is resorted to on the ground that it deepens one's understanding of the world that the professor is attempting to interpret. Teachers of modern foreign languages can always find justification for sitting around sidewalk cafés in Paris or *Bierstube* in Germany on the grounds that they are purifying their accents, and a good French accent or a good German accent is sometimes the best commodity the teacher of a modern language has to offer.

But the long summer vacation is only the most obvious fringe benefit of the college teaching profession. There is also the coveted sabbatical. The *American College Dictionary* defines a sabbatical as "(in certain universities, etc.) a year, usually every seventh year, of freedom from teaching, granted to a professor, as for study or travel." The incidence of sabbaticals, however, is by no means uniform. Some of the poorer academic institutions offer practically no sabbaticals; many of the better endowed academic institutions limit them to faculty members with tenure, although it can be argued, and has been argued, that the younger members of the faculty need freedom from teaching for study and research more than the more established members of the faculty. In some of the more lavishly endowed institutions, the sabbatical has quite lost its root meaning, and leaves for a year or a semester, with half or full pay, are granted more frequently than once in seven years. Furthermore, in a period of affluence like the present, there are available to the more promising faculty members fellowships or grants offered by one or another philanthropic foundation concerned with education and research, and the lucky faculty member may win fairly frequent periods of freedom by applying for and getting assistance of this sort which the college or university welcomes, since it relieves it of the obligation to pay the faculty member's salary during his absence.

But there are other fringe benefits besides the sabbatical and its equivalents. Most academic institutions contribute to some financial scheme that will ensure him a very modest livelihood after his retirement. Many state-supported institutions have their own pension system in which all regular employees of the state—and, in a state university, the faculty are, in a legal sense, employees of the state—participate. Most reputable private institutions require their faculty members to contribute a certain percentage of their salaries toward the purchase of an annuity and match the faculty member's contribution with an identical amount. The faculty member does not miss what he is contributing because he does not see it until it comes back to him in the form of an annuity check; the institution's contribution is actually an addition, although an invisible one, to the college teacher's salary. A further safeguard to his welfare is the chance offered by the Teachers Insurance and Annuity Association of America to assign a portion of his and the institution's contribution to an investment fund, calculated, by means of its fluctuating income, to offset the possible deterioration of the dollar value of his annuity when it falls due. For young persons entering the profession, the combination of contributions to an annuity and to an investment fund seem almost certain to offer a considerable degree of financial protection. Fairly common, also, are systems of group insurance and plans for medical and hospital care that are made available—and sometimes compulsory—for faculty members at a relatively reasonable rate, since academic personnel have proved to be among the best of insurance risks. Frequently, the amount of the insurance declines as the professor and the value of his annuity increase in years.

A somewhat less common fringe benefit available to faculty members concerns housing. Probably very few faculty members—unlike some members of academic administrations—get their living quarters rent free, although, fairly frequently, living quarters in dormitories are assigned bachelor members of the faculty or young married couples in return for duties that are sometimes nominal and sometimes onerous. The institution is likely to own property that it will rent to faculty members or, if they prefer to build homes of their own, it will lend them funds at a low rate of interest that will make possible the building of such dwellings.

The psychological rewards of college teaching are perhaps more elusive. They inevitably rise out of the professor's trio of responsibilities as teacher, as scholar, and as a member of the academic community. The relations of the teacher and the student are various. The tones with which this relationship may be invested vary widely. At the worst, the relationship may be that between a tyrant and his unhappy subjects, and even at its best there will be an element of authority in the professor-student relationship. The professor occupies a position of authority by reason of his very profession, his years, few or many, but, more particularly, his training, experience, and competence in the subject that he is teaching. The martinet will exploit the opportunities of dictatorship; the professor who does not savor power will reduce the note of authority to a minimum so that the student will scarcely be aware of it. American students are so extraordinarily well behaved, at least in the classroom, that the professor who succeeds in establishing a relaxed and amiable relation to his classes will rarely be called on to exercise the authority of a disciplinarian. Discipline may safely be entrusted to a wise and experienced Dean of Men or Dean of Students. Ideally, in my estimation, the professor in relation to his students is an older companion of greater experience and learning who treats his students as fellow travelers toward the goals of truth, understanding, and enlightenment. I doubt if there is a field of study in which this relationship cannot be established. The professor, to be sure, is, or should be, better informed about his subject than his students, and, in the more elementary courses, he inevitably has to point out gross errors in the students' work or downright mistakes in judgment. In most subjects in the humanities and the social sciences, there are no absolutely right or wrong answers to the questions raised, but, even in these subjects, the professor may be justified in designating a student's statement or judgment as decidedly and unmistakably wrong. In most cases, however, there will be a degree of truth in the student's judgment, and for that degree of truth he should be given credit. Furthermore, in matters of interpretation of a group of facts or a literary text, the acute and sensitive student, unhampered by learning and happily free from conventional responses, may have insights and detect subtleties of meaning or of style that the time-worn professor, though more experienced, may not sense or catch. For such observations and intuitions, he should be duly grateful.

Another of the psychological rewards of teaching arises from the fact that in a sense it may be regarded as one of the higher forms of play. The urge to play lies very deep in human nature, and the young human animal, as anyone would admit, learns a great deal by play that is imitative of his elders' serious activities. For the student the learning process, and for the teacher the teaching process may be, at their best, forms of play. For the student the learning process is almost bound to involve a degree of imitation of the professor's way of treating his material. The lowest form of such imitation is a parrot-like and uncomprehending repetition of the professor's operations. Seriously considered, this is learning of a very low order. Learning of a higher order of imitation involves the student's acquiring a method of working, a technique for handling material, a way of using one's mind of which the professor may furnish him the model that the student needs at the stage of his development. For the professor, teaching may also be a kind of game. I remember irritating some semiacademic person by saying that I thought that if I had amused my students I had done my duty by them. What I was suggesting was that teaching ought to be fun for both the teacher and the taught. The Puritan that lurks not far beneath the surface of most Americans is very reluctant to admit that work can ever become play. He cannot forget that one of the inescapable penalties of Adam's original sin was that he should earn his bread by the sweat of his brow. Indubitably, there are forms of work that are inescapably painful and backbreaking. But, as steam shovels have freed some men from the backbreaking labor of ditchdigging, man has shown, and continues to show, an inexhaustible ingenuity in creating labor-saving devices that enable him to escape to a degree the penalty of Adam. To put it differently, the physical labor that has created the comfortable world in which most Americans live has increased the chance for more subtle and intricate forms of intellectual work, and this intellectual work, although it is regarded superficially by nonintellectuals as not work at all, may, paradoxically, be not only work but play. The acquisition of knowledge, the transmission of knowledge, the exposure of errors, the determination of facts, and the play of ideas can and should make classroom teaching an endlessly exciting and delightful game.

Allied to the element of play in college teaching is the delight in the potentialities of educational experimentation. No matter what subject or field the professor has chosen for his life work, he will never feel—unless he lapses into an indefensible self-satisfaction—that he has arrived at the final and perfect method of teaching his subject. In any reasonably free academic institution, the professor, especially as he rises

in the ranks, and the instructor in a democratically adminis-
tered department, should find himself free to experiment with
either the subject matter or method of his courses. Since education is even more of an art than it is a science, there is an
almost infinite possibility of the forms the art may take. In
both the humanities and the social sciences, the resources in
the way of books, artifacts, and graphic and visual representa-
tions are inexhaustible; the resourceful and imaginative professor, unless he falls into the rut of repeating his performance
like a worn victrola record, will always be able to find fresh
and exciting and valuable materials with which to work. He
can always experiment with methods by shifting from the lecture to the discussion, from group research to individual research, from the seminar to the individual tutorial. If he is
lucky, he is free to organize his material in accordance with
the structural principle that seems most promising and then
abandon it for another that may, for the time being, seem
more attractive.

There are also distinct social attractions in the profession of
college teaching that may more than offset the social handicaps we have discussed in the previous chapter. These advantages arise from the professor's necessary associations with
two eternal and potentially attractive types, the professor and
the student. For, just as there are certainly unattractive professorial and student types, there are also distinctly attractive
ones.

The nature of American society is such that professors
constitute a fairly distinct class that has more or less numerous
representatives in every state of the union. Through professional signs and symbols, the members of this class are easily
recognizable by their fellow members, and an immediate sense
of fellowship and of common interests and preoccupations
comes into being. The professorial class, moreover, like the
wandering scholars of the Middle Ages, is as mobile as the

rest of American society. The professor is rare who has not taught at several colleges and universities at somewhat remote distances from each other, but, wherever he goes, he will not be long in making connections with someone he knew when he was studying or teaching at Little Neck College. The points of professorial contact arise out of the experiences that are common to the sect: the shortcomings of college presidents, the inferior scholarship of one's confrères throughout the land, the subjects of their significant research, the quality of learned journals, the chances of advancement and increases in salary, and the personalities of their colleagues and their wives.

We have already distinguished in the preceding chapter some of the less enchanting species of the genus professor. In all fairness we must insist that there are a superior number of attractive, engaging, or admirable types: the Eager Beavers, the Aesthetes, the Artists, the Scholars, the "Born Teachers," and the Elite.

The Eager Beaver is, in most respects, a very admirable member of a department and a faculty. By very nature, he is preeminently hard-working, but his work is distinguished from that of the Drone by being promising when he is young, and respectable when he becomes of scholarly age. His need for achievement is as strong as that of the undergraduate Solid Citizen, but his need can be satisfied only in the academic world. It drives him to work furiously, to read in the "literature of his subject" anything that will be grist to his productive mill; it encourages him to seize every opportunity to appear in public and to read papers. It urges him to attend every meeting of the various learned societies to which he belongs, to offer papers to be read at such meetings, and to make contact with academic personalities who may assist him in getting his scholarly or critical papers into print. His major aims in life are the making of a name for himself in the world of scholarship or criticism and the achievement of high academic rank in an Ivy League university. The chief means to these ends are incessant publication and the cultivation, if not the friendship, of people who have influence when it comes to selecting candidates to fill a good academic post. On the whole, the Eager Beaver is a rather admirable academic type. If he is not unqualifiedly admirable, the reason is that his passion for recognition makes his activity not an end in itself but hardly more than a means to an end.

To the category of Aesthetes belong the pure Aesthete and the Artist *Manqué*. Of these two types, the Aesthete is perhaps the more common. He is the individual with the temperament of the artist but without his creative power. He is much more likely than the artist to call attention to his aestheticism by eccentricities of dress or manner that strike his nonaesthetic colleagues as "affected" but that actually are natural expressions of his temperament and his taste. His characteristic response to life and the arts is not scientific or philosophical or religious but aesthetic. Whether his taste is good or bad, he is likely to manifest widely ranging interests in the arts and to attempt in his teachings to impart some of his own enthusiasm to the more sensitive members of his student audiences. Though he may be intellectually shallow, unrigorously critical, and too easily appreciative, he frequently serves as a valuable corrective to the scholarly and historical preoccupations of his colleagues. He, at least, never loses sight of the important consideration that the humanities are, or ought to be, primarily, and the social sciences at least secondarily, value subjects, and that the practitioner who is faithful to them must ever be concerned with the elucidation, revelation, and communication of values.

A close approximation to the Aesthete is the Artist *Manqué*, the man who would like to be creative but does not have the creative power he would like to have. The chief difference between the Aesthete and the Artist *Manqué* is that the former is untroubled by the urge to be creative and the latter is troubled, if not tormented, by it. He is a man who would be a writer, musician, painter, or sculptor if he had been endowed with a little more creative ability; the Artist *Manqué* bears the burden of permanent frustration. He lightens his burden least successfully when he goes on—while youth and hope last—writing unpublishable novels or painting ignominiously bad or at least not quite good pictures. He minimizes his burden most successfully perhaps when he devotes his insight and understanding of the creative process to the work of criticism. In this field—if he is not biased and embittered by his own failure—he may achieve not pseudocreation but a genuine creation, for in the eyes of time, high-minded and scrupulous criticism is only slightly less important and meaningful than the work of creation.

The Artist is perhaps the most easily distinguishable of aesthetic types. He may manifest few of the external stigmata of the aesthetic temperament; indeed, he may look and talk like an insurance salesman. He may be conspicuously inexpressive or incessantly voluble. The only essential among the differentia is his creativity. The one sure basis for his recognition is his work, and, when his productivity—for external or subjective reasons—ceases, he is, in the strict meaning of the term, no longer an Artist.

Of these aesthetic types, the one that is most likely to be gifted in teaching is the Aesthete. He is not distracted, like the Artist *Manqué*, by the creative itch nor is he seized, as the Artist is, by the compulsion to create, no matter what the opposing circumstances. As an acolyte or high priest of Beauty, the Aesthete can serve her most effectively by making converts to her, by snatching brands from the consuming fires of ignorance and provincialism, of unawareness and insensitivity. In the field of literature and the fine arts, the Artist *Manqué* is perhaps the most effective teacher of the technical elements of the art, whether it be writing, painting, or musical composition. The effectiveness of the Artist as a teacher is by no means dependent on the quantity or quality of his productivity. Of the skills and processes that make his artistic productions distinguished, he may be unaware or at least incapable of expression and communication. The Artist's chief contribution to the academic community—and it is an extremely important one—is the example given by his presence of the actual creative process, of the absorption of a gifted personality in the process of creation, of the fact—obvious but frequently neglected by academic historians and scholars—that the arts did not come to an end in 1500 or 1800 or even 1900, but that their creation goes on, in fair weather or foul, significantly or insignificantly. The Artist in the academic community is the symbol of the endlessness of the living process of artistic creation, a challenging witness to the fact that art is not merely the subject matter for historical and critical scrutiny or defenseless material to be used in the manufacture of theses and scholarly articles, but a way of life, a form of knowledge, a medium of vision and insight and wisdom.

Another admirable, if not always superficially delightful, professorial type is the Scholar. He is characterized by his devotion to research and the methods of research, to the accumulation of material and its systematic presentation with serried footnotes and bibliographies. At his worst, the Scholar is hardly distinguishable from the Drone, immersed in minutiae, hopelessly lost in the eternal process of collecting and arranging material and progressively incapable of putting his accumulated material to any significant use. At his best, he is moved by one of the noblest of human motives—the passion for extending the bounds of knowledge. His consuming objective is the discovery of the whole truth with respect to the subject he has chosen for investigation. To this end, he is indefatigable in the collection of all the facts that may be relevant to a solution of his problem. His method is the exploration of every avenue that may lead to facts that have been hitherto unobserved or long lost sight of. Even seemingly trivial or apparently irrelevant facts may ultimately prove significant and crucial for the solution of his problem. In the collection, the weighing, the organizing of facts and the marshaling of arguments, he aims at the utmost precision and the soundest logic. If he is judicious in his choice of his problem, unremittingly assiduous in working toward its solution, and fastidious in the evaluation of evidence, he may emerge with a pattern of facts, a display of illuminating ideas, or a soundly demonstrated and fresh judgment that will indeed constitute a genuine contribution to knowledge.

The Scholar's pure devotion to the discovery of the truth may have more objective rewards than his own satisfaction in having solved a difficult problem. As the results of his researches are published and recognized, not only may he feel the natural pleasure that arises from the establishment of facts, the elucidation of ideas, and the clarification of values in the field to which he has chosen to devote his scholarly life, but he may legitimately enjoy the recognition that comes to him as an authority in his field, one whose experience and judgment are appealed to by younger and less seasoned workers.

An even more attractive professorial type is the "Born Teacher," the person who flourishes most in his relations with students in and out of the classroom, who expresses himself most potently in his devotion to the fine art of teaching, and who, at his best, achieves something of the artist's creativity in his skill in bringing about a vital relationship between the student and what the student is learning or being taught. If the Aesthete is marked by some of the characteristics of the Artist, the "Born Teacher" is distinguished by some of the characteristics of the actor on the one hand and the preacher on the other. Like the actor, he is gifted with platform skills; his personality is so plastic that it is possible for him to achieve a temporary but more or less complete identification of himself with the subject or the author he is discussing. He handles his voice effectively; he may even become famous—as "Copey" of Harvard did—as a public reader. He is sensitive to the reactions of his audience, knows how to play upon them, and is able to make effective patterns and juxtapositions of the personalities in his group of auditors. Like the actor, he has a sense of timing, a flare for the effective use of stage properties, and a wide range of tones from the casual and inconsequential to the ironical and dramatic. But the "Born Teacher" is less self-centered than the actor, more genuinely outgoing, more personally distinct. Although, like the actor with the text of the play, he uses the subject matter of his field as raw material for his performance, the "Born Teacher" feels not only an aesthetic but a moral responsibility to the subject matter with which he is working and also to the audience to whom he is presenting this subject matter. Like the true pastor, he has a "cure of souls." He is concerned with his students not merely as minds but as men, not as points on the sliding scale of intellectual accomplishment but as human beings with personalities that are curiously complex blends of assets and liabilities, that are bundles of potentialities. Like the pastor, he furnishes—sometimes unwittingly—a kind of norm for behavior and manners, a model, however imperfect, of devotion to the nobler ends of which the human animal dreams and in the attainment of which he is, perhaps fitfully, engaged.

The classification of professorial types just completed is obviously more applicable to members of departments of literature, the fine arts, and music than to members of history or philosophy departments. In these latter disciplines, however, the basic distinction between the teacher and the scholar holds good. Historians might well be classified in terms of the breadth or the narrowness of their conception of history. The more "scholarly" the historian, the narrower his interests are likely to be. The broader his interests, the greater the likelihood of his being an inspiring and widely influential teacher. The most broad-minded historians are those who regard all that has happened as their province, who conceive of history as significant in proportion to its inclusiveness, and who have a capacity for synthesizing not only the dynastic, military, and political but also the social, aesthetic, religious, and philosophical elements in a culture into large and meaningful patterns.

It is also possible to distinguish a number of types of professorial philosophers. The specialist in this area is likely to devote himself exclusively to the interpretation of a particular philosopher (and he may be justified when the philosopher is a major figure like Plato or Whitehead) or to the cultivation of a particular branch of philosophy: epistemology, metaphysics, logic, aesthetics, or ethics. A rather rare type among academic philosophers is the man who attempts to create a philosophical system of his own. If he is sufficiently brilliant and original, he may come—as Whitehead did—to have an influence far beyond that of the classroom; he may indeed become an international figure.

The most commonly recurrent type of academic philosopher is the man who does not attempt to work out his own philosophical system or to devote himself to a particular philosopher or branch of philosophy, but who concerns himself with elucidating sympathetically but critically the works of the great philosophers from Plato and Aristotle down to the present. A man who, in a sense, takes all philosophy as his province, may, in the course of the years, become a widely and deeply informed and cultivated person who can bring his philosophical insights to bear on all the other subjects in the college curriculum and at his best can serve as a mediator between one subject and another. Most professors outside the Department of Philosophy are inadequately trained in the philosophical implications of their subject, and may in fact be unaware that they are operating on the basis of untrustworthy philosophical assumptions. The broadly interested and widely read and tactful professor of philosophy can often clarify and illuminate the goal and function of subjects that are not his own private preserve. Since the philosopher operates on a level of abstraction far higher than that of the historian, he can, at his best, serve as elucidator, classifier, and systematizer of all the other subjects in the college or university curriculum.

As a teacher, moreover, the philosopher demonstrates more clearly than the members of any other department in the college the close relation between teaching and preaching. For, whether or not he is overtly the propagandist for a particular school of philosophy, he is much more likely to be conscious of his own philosophical orientation than the professor of English or history or economics, and, even when he does not actively and vigorously proselytize, he and his personality express his philosophy implicitly and make converts, with or without the expenditure of conscious effort. Since the academic philosopher is or may be dealing with basic values, he has a chance of being a profound and enduring influence on the thoughts and actions of his students.

It is frequently from the ranks of the academic philosophers that there emerges the rarest and, in some respects, the most precious, if not always the most immediately attractive of professorial types, those who compose the Elite, the pure Intellectuals, the men with genuinely creative minds. The infrequency with which this type appears may be accounted for by the fact that the academic mind, although it is supposed to be intellectually adventuresome, actually limits its explorations to relatively safe and placid waters. The academic world does not often encourage or welcome or stimulate profoundly provocative or fundamentally disturbing ideas. The genuinely creative Intellectual, furthermore, is likely to be profoundly impatient of academic rules and regulations and of the college's insistence on the relatively unimportant details of pedagogy and of scholarship. He is likely to be very disturbing to administrative officials who believe it to be their responsibility to practice the rituals laid down by the college's rules and regulations. In a large university the creative Intellectual may be permitted to go his way and to ignore the responsibilities imposed on lesser minds. In a small college, on the other hand, the pure Intellectual, if he appears, is likely to be barely tolerated and, if possible, quietly eliminated. The realization that the ideas that have most profoundly influenced the modern mind have usually not come from professors points up the fundamentally conservative, nonrevolutionary character of most of our institutions of higher education.

The social advantages of college teaching as a profession are not limited to those that arise from the professor's contacts with the more attractive professorial types in and out of his own department. For some college teachers, a more weighty social advantage arises out of their ever renewed contacts with some of the more attractive types of students. Although, as we have pointed out, there may be in a variegated student body types as unappealing as Drips, Thugs, Pseudointellectuals, and Anonymities, and although the Solid Citizens promise a rather dubious return on the professor's investment of time and energy, there are student types contact with whom constitutes one of the more refreshing aspects of the professor's life, perhaps ultimately its most rewarding aspect. Of these more attractive types, it may be worth while to distinguish the Hearties, the Grinds, the embryonic Artists, and the Intellectual Elite.

A superficial observer might very well confuse the Solid Citizens and the Hearties, since physically they bear a marked resemblance to each other. The Hearty differs from the Solid Citizen in a certain modest capacity to become interested in the life of the mind and of the spirit. There is in him a stirring of intellectual curiosity, an embryonic sensibility that can be appealed to, and that may very well develop, at least for a short time, into an active and lively intellectual and aesthetic interest. In some ways the Hearty offers the most interesting challenge to the college teacher, who must make a special effort to get at the Hearty's potentials and to bring out into the light and encourage the development of those sensibilities and curiosities and insights that his heartiness has led him to repress or at least not to express.

Less attractive but more immediately responsive to the teacher's effort is the Grind. The epithet, of course, is not the victim's choice; it is a term by means of which the less intellectual and less industrious students indicate their disapprobation of what seems to them an unpleasantly excessive devotion to the demands of the college curriculum. The college teacher, on the other hand, denominates the Grind as diligent, hard-working, serious, teachable. The Grind is marked by a tremendous need for achievement, but for some reason he cannot satisfy his need—as other undergraduates do—by success and recognition in athletics or some other extracurricular activity.

The Aesthetes and Artists on the faculty will not find it difficult to discover embryonic Artists among their students. Here, as on the professional level, there is a wide range between the Aesthete who is satisfied with the appreciation of works of art, through the students who hope to become Artists but never will, to the student who has genuine creative powers that with luck may make him a practicing Artist. They will naturally gravitate to the subjects that lend themselves to the aesthetic approach: literature, music, and the fine arts. To teachers in these fields, such students are the most responsive and rewarding, and a close relationship between master and disciple may contribute substantially to the education of both. The most gifted of them—those who show signs of possessing genuine creativity—are among the most exciting and satisfying of the college teacher's clients.

The rarest of attractive student types, as of faculty types, is the Intellectual, the student with a genuinely creative mind, a mind that generates fresh, illuminating, and original ideas as distinct from producing works of literary and visual art. The identification of the embryonic Intellectual among undergraduates is a by no means easy task; if it is difficult to draw the line between genius and madness, it is not easy to draw the line between the Pseudointellectual and the Intellectual. In any case even the genuinely creative mind, at this early stage, is likely to find itself at odds with the intellectual conformity that characterizes second-rate academic minds and second-rate academic institutions. In the future, however, if his creative intelligence flowers, he may be one of the few reasons why his alma mater is favorably known among those who recognize first-rate intellectual creativity.

But however lucky or unlucky the professor may be in his contact with undergraduates, no matter how diverse the undergraduates may be with whom the professor has the opportunity or obligation to associate, there is always the undeniable advantage that they are all young and offer him the opportunity to immerse himself again and again in the stream of unending youth—a professor's unique privilege. The inexhaustible attraction of the undergraduate is his youth with the vestiges of dewy innocence, particularly in freshmen, the clearness of vision, the alert curiosity, the eagerness to extend and deepen and understand whatever experience and books may offer him.

The most irresistible of the undergraduate's attractions is the sense he gives of unexplored and unrealized potentialities. The college teacher, as he inevitably ages, may develop the sense that his own potentialities have defined themselves or, within his powers, have been realized. He may, therefore, get a profound vicarious satisfaction out of his efforts to point his students' way to the development of potentialities that, perhaps a little ruefully, he acknowledges that he himself does not have. Among the professor's most enduring satisfactions are the pleasure and the pride he takes in the later careers of students to whose early training he may have contributed and whose intellectual ambition he may have aroused or encouraged. Since scholarly knowledge is cumulative, the professor may conceive of his disciples as contributing their shares to building the tower of truth whose foundations he may himself have assisted in solidifying. The scholarly standards he has attempted to exemplify, the intellectual and moral qualities he has striven to embody, will, he hopes, furnish a model, however faulty, that the most brilliant of his followers may perfect.

Another undeniable advantage of college teaching as a profession is that it is not a dead-end road; it offers inexhaustible opportunities for the professor's own growth and development. The growth may take the form of increased knowledge or deepened wisdom. If the teacher is a specialist—and every good teacher should be a specialist in some area of learning, however minute—he knows very well that he can never get to know all there is to know about his specialty. If he wants to avoid the static horror of intellectual death, he can endeavor constantly not only to master the impressive bulk of facts that he and others have already discovered but to bring to light facts that no other specialist in the field has observed. Furthermore, he is repeatedly challenged to integrate new facts with old, and to modify the patterns of interpretation that he has constructed and that he must re-order in the light of newly discovered facts. But, since the good teacher is not only a specialist but an intelligent amateur, there are open to him endless possibilities that will enrich his understanding of his own subject by extending its boundaries to include relevant facts and ideas from related disciplines and subject matters. For the philosopher and the historian, no fact, no opinion, no judgment that can be snatched from devouring time need be irrelevant to his own study and understanding. For the teacher of literature, music, or the fine arts, psychology, philosophy, or history may enrich his understanding of the culture out of which the literature and art have flowered. He may also deepen his insight and wisdom not only by the contemplation and analysis of the experience of himself and his friends but by contact with the great thinkers of every age: Plato, Aristotle, Dante, Shakespeare, Tolstoy, Dostoevski, and Whitehead.

For the teacher who is aware of the potentialities of his profession, the classroom, with its more or less captive audience, offers, even more satisfactorily than the pulpit or the political rostrum, the paradox of escape and confrontation. The banal charge that the college teacher escapes from the pressures and demands of "real" life by taking refuge in the ivory tower of the classroom is baseless. The more neurotic professorial types, one must admit, may find the academic community a happy nursery for their infantile and immature preoccupations, and the relatively normal college professor may temporarily and happily escape in the classroom from the inevitable annoyances incidental to going on living: the butcher's bill, the holes in the children's shoes, even the anxieties and agonies inseparable from the life of the heart. But the classroom in a genuinely liberal institution of higher learning is completely free from the strait-jackets of doctrine that may limit the intellectual gestures of the minister or the priest and

from the partisan bias and vulgarization that are inseparable
from political campaigning. At its best, the classroom is not
in any profound or searching sense an escape from life; instead, it is a point of vantage with a serene and cloudless
climate that encourages a confrontation of life, an exploration of its potentialities, a free and uninhibited probing into
its meaning and its mystery. In the classroom, life is confronted at a depth and with an intensity that the superficiali-
ties, the need for compromise, and the brutalities of the outer
world discourage or make impossible.

But the greatest attraction of college teaching as a profession is the hope it inspires that it may contribute significantly
to the education of generation after generation of students.
Here, to be sure, it is all important to avoid the deceptions
engendered by self-love. As Philip E. Jacobs has written: "By
and large the impact of the teacher the students consider good
is indistinguishable from that of the poor one—at least in
terms of his influence on the student's values. *Some* teachers,
however, assert a powerful influence on *some* students, even
to the point of causing particular students to adopt new and
usually more socially responsible goals. It is perhaps significant that faculty members having this power are likely to be
those whose value-commitments are openly expressed and
who are outgoing and warm in their student relationships." *
Inevitably, too, the teacher is often left in utter ignorance of
his enduring influence on many students. Although he may be
disconcerted to discover that students are inclined to remember his casual witticisms rather than his more serious observations, he may sometimes learn to his astonishment that he has
furnished an example or model for someone whose existence
he has almost forgotten. Fortunately, however, he will occasionally be rewarded by a student's grateful testimony to the

* *Changing Values in College* (New York: Harper and Brothers, 1957),
pp. 7–8.

contribution he has made to his knowledge and understanding. But seed cast even on stony ground may bear precious, if invisible, fruit.

The college professor lives in the hope that, at the most elementary level, he may have trained his students in the technique of the ways and means of discovering what is already dependably known about whatever subject the student is interested in, and also in sound logical processes of thought, in orderly and rational methods of work, and in the discrimination between what is and what is not evidence.

His abiding faith is that he may contribute significantly to his students' conversion from falsehood to truth, from fiction to fact, from prejudice to tolerance, from light to darkness, from ignorance to knowledge, from folly to wisdom.